D0390130

But Dad!

But Dad!

A Survival Guide for Single Fathers of Tween and Teen Daughters

Gretchen Gross

and

Patricia Livingston

ROWMAN & LITTLEFIELD PUBLISHERS, INC.

Lanham • Boulder • New York • Toronto • Plymouth, UK

Published by Rowman & Littlefield Publishers, Inc.
A wholly owned subsidiary of The Rowman & Littlefield Publishing Group, Inc.
4501 Forbes Boulevard, Suite 200, Lanham, Maryland 20706
www.rowman.com

Estover Road, Plymouth PL6 7PY, United Kingdom

Distributed by National Book Network

Copyright © 2012 by Rowman & Littlefield Publishers, Inc.

All rights reserved. No part of this book may be reproduced in any form or by any electronic or mechanical means, including information storage and retrieval systems, without written permission from the publisher, except by a reviewer who may quote passages in a review.

British Library Cataloguing in Publication Information Available

Library of Congress Cataloging-in-Publication Data
Gross, Gretchen, 1959–
    But dad! : a survival guide for single fathers of tween and teen daughters / Gretchen Gross and Patricia Livingston.
        p. cm.
    Includes bibliographical references and index.
    ISBN 978-1-4422-1267-1 (pbk. : alk. paper)—ISBN 978-1-4422-1268-8 (ebook)
    1. Single fathers. 2. Parenting. 3. Teenage girls. 4. Fathers and daughters.
    I. Livingston, Patricia, 1952– II. Title.
    HQ759.915.G76 2012
    306.874'22—dc23   2011044670

∞™ The paper used in this publication meets the minimum requirements of American National Standard for Information Sciences—Permanence of Paper for Printed Library Materials, ANSI/NISO Z39.48-1992.

Printed in the United States of America

To my daughter, Gia, who has taught me everything I know about being a mother.

G.G.

To my parents, Pat and George, for your unconditional love and support through thick and thin.

P.L.

Contents

Foreword

R AISING CHILDREN is difficult under the best circumstances. We all believe that there are better and worse ways to parent. That's why most parents try so hard to get it right. Most of us hope that our own experience, common sense, and the advice of trusted friends will be enough to make us successful as parents. We cannot escape the fact that parenting and relationships are extremely complex. In an age of information, it may seem surprising that the entire process is so frail.

But there are experts on child development, relationships, and families. Psychologists, social workers, and other social scientists have learned a great deal. Therapists and medical professionals who work with families and children gain enormous experience and insight into the needs and reactions of children and parents—under both "ordinary" family circumstances and extraordinary parenting challenges.

Many of us will look to these experts for guidance.

Written help can reassure us that our observations are sensible. We are comforted to know that others have faced the same difficulties. We may be embarrassed to ask certain questions, or we may not even be sure what questions to ask. And we like to hear what experts say. Having gathered a lot of information, we can piece it together in a way that makes sense to us, we can avoid some pitfalls that we had not thought about, and we can keep our heads clear so that we make the best judgments available.

As difficult as parenting may be, raising a daughter as a single father is even more challenging. There may be very little experience related to raising a daughter—not even a sister in the father's past. Males and females sometimes have different ways of thinking, so there is a gender gap to overcome. Together with divorce or the death of the mother, there are additional traumas that complicate the task. All of these factors add to the normal challenges of parenting.

Our authors are in a very good position to assist a single father. They have been daughters themselves, so they are aware of the needs of girls at this age. They are both single mothers who have raised daughters. They have a professional background and have had considerable opportunity to learn about the needs of children and parents in many different situations. Most importantly, they have given much thought to what a father would need to know as a single parent.

Most parents do not have the time and ability to become experts on child development. At the same time, parenting cannot be simplified to a simple list of tasks. This book explains the developmental issues, provides strategies for dealing with the challenges that both fathers and daughters face in their respective roles, and then makes practical recommendations for dads—advice they can use from women who are "in the know" both personally and professionally. The book will cultivate understanding of girls' needs while giving clear and specific guidance for handling particular situations. For a father who may not know what is in the mind of a girl of this age, the information found here will offer some understanding. The balance of information is just right.

This book will help you to address the special challenges of raising a tween or teenage daughter as a single father. It is both serious and funny, both friendly and firm, and both knowledgeable and practical.

You're probably going to find *But Dad! A Survival Guide for Single Fathers of Tween and Teen Daughters* both informative and enjoyable. Good luck to you and your daughter(s)!

Robert Pierattini, M.D., professor and chair
University of Vermont Department of Psychiatry

Acknowledgments

SPECIAL THANKS go to my parents, Peg Sorgio and Stan Moses. This adventure started with you and I'm so grateful for all I have learned. To the single dads, Michael, Doug, Tim, John, and more, who offered insight, encouragement, proofreadings, comments, and support, we thank you. Special thanks to Pat Livingston, who couldn't be a better coauthor and friend, whose brother, Tom Livingston, contributed tirelessly to long hours of work on our index. Finally to Suzanne Staszak-Silva and Julia Loy, our editors, who trust in this project and helped shepherd it to print, we are so grateful.

G.G.

IWANT TO further acknowledge my brother, Tom, for his ongoing encouragement and stellar job on our index. We valued your patience, guidance, and professionalism throughout this project.

Emma and Charlie—what can I say? You knew I could do this and never let me doubt myself. Thanks for cooking the fabulous meals and patiently troubleshooting innumerable computer glitches! I'm so proud of you both!

And, of course, thank you, Gretchen, for being there for me and for pushing this project along!

P.L.

Can This Book Help You Raise Your Daughter?

IT'S NOT a stretch to say that through the course of history, men have been flummoxed, perplexed, mystified, and completely confused by women. As a single dad of daughters who are about to enter or are smack dab in the middle of puberty, you feel like a Giant's outfielder during game 3 of the 1989 World Series. You've heard the small scraping sounds like nails on a chalkboard, felt the slight ground tremors. Like the Giants, the Athletics, and the thousands of fans in the stands, you know "it" is coming but don't yet know what "it" is or how much damage might be done. The ground underneath you is shifting.

Puberty is, at best, a hugely complex process for both boys and girls. The rate of change, and its meanings, has shifted for young women. Currently the age of onset of puberty hovers around ten years old. This means that internal hormonal shifts begin even earlier. The changes are biological, sexual, physical, emotional, and social. It's big stuff and the more any parent knows about it, the better. So here is one book, a single resource, that you can keep on your nightstand, in the garage, on the workbench, in your computer case, or wherever you want, ready whenever you need it, so you can be a prepared, have some questions answered, and be a great dad to your daughter.

And let's face it: this can be as rocky a time for moms and dads as it is for young girls. The better prepared you are, the easier this passage will be for both of you and any other close family members who live with you.

You can now, whenever you want and wherever you choose, tweak your fathering skills by flipping to the chapter of your choice. Imagine this. Within days, your daughters will start saying, "Gosh Dad, you're really growing and learning as a father! You're the best! I love it that you're learning more about me." The reason we said "imagine" is because that scenario will occur only in your imagination. If your daughter sees this book, she'll likely respond with something quite opposite. Something more along the lines of "That book just looks stupid, Dad. Why did you even buy it? Please don't even say the word *cramps* around me. That's disgusting. Don't think you'll find anything in that book that will work on me!" Teens don't think you can learn anything about them in any book. As the penguins in the movie *Madagascar* said, "Smile and nod, boys, smile and nod."

Here's what you won't find in this book: psychobabble (well, not too much), charts, or useless graphs. You won't need a degree in sociology, psychology, or developmental biology to get through these chapters. All you need is an interest in being the best dad possible to your daughter as she rocks and rolls through some of the more challenging days of her life.

You will find this a simple book with easy access to what you want to know. This is the *Consumer's Digest* on daughters, the playbook on puberty, the racing sheets on raising daughters. When you really need help, you can crack this book, find the chapter that answers your questions, and find out all you want and need to know on any given topic related to single parenting a young girl. It's just that easy. After feeling completely inept, as all parents do when dealing with preteen and teen daughters, you will: Step 1: curse under your breath, mad at yourself that you didn't see that argument or conversation coming, and you swear to do it better next time so you . . . Step 2: pull this book off your bedside table and turn to the chapter dealing with the issue de jour, and you . . . Step 3: read, learn, and say, "Why didn't someone tell me about this before? I won't make that mistake again." That's how you use this book.

Let's cut to the chase and talk about why you should take our word in any of this. A few weeks ago at a party, a male friend asked, "Why should a guy listen to two women tell him how to be a good dad? You've never been a dad. Isn't that like me telling you about childbirth?" This friend is a major in the military, has flown F-16s, has a significant intellect, and is now a pilot for a major airline. I said, "Mark, if I wanted to learn how to fly, I'd learn from someone like you. Someone who's been there, done that, and knows the details about how to stay in the air rather than crash and burn. I mean sure, I've been in a plane. I know to locate the emergency exits. Does that make me well prepared to head to the flight deck?" After puffing up his chest a bit from all the compliments, he paused. Mark knows his stuff. I'd feel safe in a plane with him at the stick. "So follow me, Mark. If you needed to know about cramps, tampons, mood swings, dating boys, middle school girl cliques, throwing a great slumber party, and when is it okay to start to wear makeup, who would you ask?" He paused for a moment, looked thoughtful, then responded, "Got it. Want a beer?" Mark and his wife have four sons. His wife, Penny, was smiling and shaking her head. "Mark, when someone needed to talk to Geoff about his voice cracking, we sent you in. When Chris needed some support after he got hurt and couldn't play ball, when he thought his world had ended, who talked to him night after night? There's a lot I can do as a mom, but we both know there's stuff you just know better. And yeah, if you weren't home, or were deployed, I'd do it. But I'd do it with your help." Mark went back to his discussion about his deep desire to buy a Porsche 911 for his impending midlife crisis, while Penny and I smiled and shook our heads. There you have it. The reason why we wrote this book is because women have the inside track on girl stuff. We know the secrets. We've got the 411 on pads, tampons, cramps, broken girl hearts, zit creams, and shaving legs, why a girl might miss her mom and what to do about it, eating disorders, and what to say about dating besides, "I know what boys want, honey, and you can't go out with him!"

Pat and I have both raised daughters and co-parented with exes. So we have a sense of what men know, want to know, and what they think they know but need some help with. Because we've had to, women know how to get blood stains out of bed sheets, how to talk to daughters about dating and sex, and how to help her pick out clothes that are age appropriate for that upcoming bar mitzvah. We know the difference between hormonal mood swings and bad behavior. We understand the complexities (and really, they are complexities) between mini- and maxi-pads, and maxi-pads with wings, and which are the most comfortable under leggings.

The more you understand about girls in this age group, what they want, what they need, what's going on, what they aren't telling you, and what you would rather not ask your ex, your mom, or the new woman you're dating, the better father you'll be and the more prepared you'll be for the changes of adolescence.

As parents, we're all at wit's end more often than we care to admit. When we want some answers, we don't want to read through chapters and chapters on Oedipal issues in adolescence or family dynamics as they affect only children. We want quick, clean information from someone we trust, and can maybe laugh along with. That's why this book is chock full of info, short on theory, and long on kitchen table wisdom with a dash of necessary humor.

We include references if you want to read more deeply into topics. But we also want to just give you the "quick and simple" so you have fewer moments of feeling like you're flopping around on the deck as your teen daughter walks away. So let's talk about you for a minute.

Why Fathers Matter So Much

Have you noticed that there are plenty of books about mothers and daughters? In her book *Mothers and Daughters during Adolescence*, Teri Apter writes, "The strange, disturbing, and sad picture seems to be that during the daughter's adolescence, the distance between them increases." Sadly, the "them" she talks about is fathers and daughters. On its own, this is a distressing observation. When you think about this from the perspective of single fatherhood, it's awful. Since when did fathers get marginalized, pushed off to the side, rendered invisible? Ironically, if you do happen to be a research hound, you'll find the data on the importance of fathers. Sadly, this information has not leaked into the everyday life as much as it should. The truth is dads are incredibly important to the development of healthy daughters. Dads' level of involvement with their daughters is positively correlated to their daughter's level of success at work and their overall sense of comfort and mastery of the world around them. That sounds pretty essential to us. You are important. As a single dad, your time with your daughter is more important than ever.

Please don't think we're suggesting you become mothers, because we're not. Here's what we know about fathers and their patterns of interacting with their children. Fathers are more involved with the physical play and activities of both sons and daughters. You're more likely to coach their teams, take them skiing, toss a ball around. Your activities are more often located outside the house and in outdoor activities. You understand that in playing sports, the skill of risk taking—pushing oneself beyond the same old, same old—is honed. You are less worried about injury. If you've ever watched a mother and father with a toddler, you'll notice things. A mother monitors the child more closely and stays closer. She speaks softer and her movements are slower. In swoops Dad. He picks up the toddler while on a run, bustles her under his arm like a sack of flower, and she is laughing her head off. He picks up speed and whirls her around while they both laugh. Mom, meanwhile, is holding her hand on her mouth, waiting for someone to fall and start crying. Likewise, children interact differently with their dads. In Doucet's article, one dad is quoted as saying, "They climb all over me! I am the play structure!" We know we do it differently, moms and dads. And both of us bring important things to the table. When we are under the same roof and getting along well, there is a balance. The kids get both. But when a family divorces or when a mom dies, much falls on the parent the kids are with, when they're with them.

Male ways of connecting are also famously different. Maybe you are from Mars, but we sure as heck are not from Venus. We do, however, generally want to talk more, connect more, process more, and it's all about the relationship. Men, as we know, move to solve problems as quickly as possible. You value social hierarchy and are usually perfectly content to compete to win, whether it's in the sales force, on the golf course, or with your kids when you're tossing a ball around. So when a teen girl, in the middle of some sort of struggle, is with her dad and wants some help, the interaction might go something like this:

DAUGHTER: Dad, I have a problem.

DAD: What's that, sweetie?

DAUGHTER: I've got four projects due this week and I won't get them all done on time. I want to keep my grades up. I'm just worried.

DAD: No problem. Let's just sit with a calendar and set up a schedule. Okay, so tomorrow night you don't have soccer practice so you can work on the science stuff for three hours. You should be able to get it done in that time. So see, that's Monday!

DAUGHTER: Yeah, Dad, I get that. I'm just worried.

DAD: No need to be worried, honey! Tuesday, let's look at Tuesday, How much time do you have to work on it on Tuesday?

DAUGHTER: No, Dad. You're not listening. I'm really worried about getting this done.

And so on and so on and so on. You've got a clear path to a solution, but she doesn't seem to see that. In fact, she seems to keep getting more emotional and getting more worried. In this situation and possibly more like it, you're doing what men do well. You're providing a solution to a problem. She wants you to think like her and offer some comfort, a calm ear, and some reassurance. In short, she craves connection. She probably already has some level of solution worked up in her head, so she's frustrated that you are focusing on that. That's not what's important. What's important is that you know she's nervous. She feels shaky and wants someone to lean on. You want to take her distress away and you have a darn good strategy to help her accomplish those goals, but she's not happy with that. And maybe this escalates even more. Maybe she starts to cry and leaves the kitchen table where you were camped out and says, "You just don't get it, Dad. You just don't get it!"

Huh? You got it and you offered help. What's up with her? Must be hormonal. Aw geeze, that again? It's so much easier with boys. And it just may be easier because you speak the same language, and look for the same things. Much like moms and daughters. The internal music is similar so we know the steps, or at least the dance we're dancing in any particular moment.

Divorce and the
Other *D*—Deployment

Divorce

Let's just say it. Divorce stinks. The whole process seems to support anger and adversity. The woman you loved became your opponent. The children may have become part of the dividing process. Maybe they chose sides and are angry at Mom or Dad or both. You're so tired of figuring out how many nights at what home equals what child support amount. Who pays what to whom? Who has the kids on what nights, and who has legal custody, and what does visitation look like? You and your ex have fought, ground it out, said nasty things, and sent flaming arrows over each other's walls. It's hard to believe that you ever liked this person, let alone believed you could cooperate well enough to be parents together. But you did like and love this person, and you did father a child with her. When there are children involved, that's important to remember.

If your divorce was difficult and fairly recent, you might be sad. Angry. Relieved. Scared. Confused. Liberated. At this moment your daughters might be sad. Angry. Relieved. Scared. Wondering. Most of all they are just hoping that the fighting, yelling, and cold shoulders are behind them. The custody fight may be ongoing or you may have to return to court in a while to change child support payment or to re-petition the court. Know this. The longer the court battles go on, the poorer you get, the less energy you have for your children, the more the children see and hear you be frustrated and angry and exhausted. At some point you will step back and ask, "Am I interested in putting my monetary and emotional resources into the court system anymore?" Some people keep going to court to stay in one another's lives, as odd as that sounds, or to keep sticking it to their ex. The kids know about the court situation. It makes them tense. When the *Boston Globe* ran Anne Jarell's article called "The Daddy Track," one father who is also a lawyer who has seen custody battles from both sides of the fence said, "If parents realized the emotional turmoil and anguish they were causing their children, they'd find a way to settle their differences and stay out of court."

Getting custody, even if it's partial custody, of your daughter may mean some significant changes for you. You may need to increase your income if the expenses increase. You may get child support if their mom earns more or has the children for less time than you do. More and more courts are open to realizing that some mothers are not able to fulfill parenting responsibilities because of mental instability, drug addiction, or even military deployment.

Over 30,000 mothers have been deployed to Iraq and Afghanistan since the war started. In some cases, the fathers remain as the primary caregivers. In this situation the stressors on the family are significantly different, when a mom is in a war zone. But let's focus now on divorce.

Your Marriage Is Over. Your Job Is Not!

Arrrrggghhh. You might be having a visceral reaction just thinking about your ex. How could you ever have wanted to be a parent with her? The divorce process focuses on the failures in your marriage. Sometimes the process works because it's so damn difficult, painful, and exhausting that it wears you down and you are completely ready to sign and let go. But this is not the dissolution of a business partnership; this is the end of a family, and the kids are smack dab in the middle of that. So try to actively remind yourself that you loved your ex, thought she was wonderful and would be a great mom. The more you can do this, no matter how painful or how angry you get, the better a dad you'll be to your daughters. Do you know why? Well, there's a whole body of psychological theory that reminds us that we are, at stages of our lives, deeply connected to the parent of the same gender. Girls model after their mothers. They internalize an aspect of her. They are deeply connected and, in some ways, very similar. So what you say about her mom, or women in general, she hears you saying about her. If she's heterosexual, she'll eventually look for a similar man to you. If you are kind and respectful to women, she'll seek that in a partner. If you blame your ex, put her down in front of your daughter, she'll think that's acceptable behavior and will look for those features later in life.

Everything, positive or negative, that you say about your ex/her mom, she hears as what you think and say about her. So when you vent your anger at your ex to the kids, that's friendly fire. You're aiming at Mom and it ricochets right back to the girl sitting in the passenger seat of your car. After all, that child just really wants to go about her business of loving you both, fighting with you both, getting your approval, messing with your head, and all the other normal things that kids do. Try as hard as you can to not vent to the children or within earshot. This takes awareness and some control but you love your kids and you can do this. Because none of us is perfect, you'll make a mistake. You'll be so frustrated you say something before you realize who's in the next room on the couch with little ears perked. When that happens, immediately take responsibility. Say, "Honey, I'm sorry. I was frustrated with something, but I shouldn't have said it to you or around you. My error. I will try as hard as I can to not do it again." Don't make excuses like, "But your mother just did the stupidest thing. . . . She always. . . ." Just pause, recognize that you crossed that big line in the sand by venting to your kid, and apologize.

The truth about divorce is that is it an end to a marriage, not an end to a co-parenting relationship, even if you have full custody. Do not make your daughter pay for your anger at her mom, or the failure of the marriage. *Your ex is still her mother.* She is still an important part of the family in your daughter's eyes. As Dad, you need to take your anger, frustration, and sadness and leave them outside of your relationship with your kids. There is a wonderful saying that goes like this: *Love your child more than you hate your ex.* We know this is sometimes easier said than done. Drop-offs are heated. Phone calls are challenging. School meetings are difficult. But, always, for the sake of your kids, make the space in your relationship with them a "no fly zone" for anger about your ex. Here are a few very concrete suggestions:

- Try really hard not to have angry phone conversations with their mom in front of them. Simply say, "I won't talk about that now. We can e-mail or set up another time." If this doesn't work, it's really okay to end the phone call. Some couples find that setting a date and time to talk enables them to have privacy and hash things out away from the kids.
- Put some physical space between you and your ex if that will help. Sit on different ends of the bleachers at soccer, talk with other parents at school events if the tension is high.

- When you are both attending an event like a school play or game, be clear that your daughter is scoping both of you out. And her job is to be a kid, not an air-traffic controller. Show her that she can focus on the game, her lines, or her musical part and without worrying about her mom and dad getting into a brawl in row C. Do this by being present to her activity. Watch her because, we promise, she's watching you. Laugh at her lines, cheer her on from the sidelines, applaud wildly after she's finished competing or reading her poem.

- Fake nice with the ex if you need to. You've done it before in meetings— fake a light mood. Fake a wave to your ex's parents, who are also there to support your daughter. Only you know you're faking it and you get good dad points. Your daughter will just know that she can concentrate on the goal, on her part in the play, and not have to worry about breaking up a fight or hiding backstage to avoid the anger. As we've said, but can't stress enough, don't badmouth your ex in front of her. If you can't respond neutrally ("Did you tell Mom about your game?") or positively ("Mom would love to watch you practice. Did you call and ask if she wants to come?"), then don't say a thing. Seal your mouth closed with crazy glue. Here's a clue, if you hear yourself talking in negative generalizations about Mom—"She's *never* on time. She's *always* got to be right"—you're likely on shaky ground. If, on the other hand you're saying things like, "Mom has always loved you. She's always proud of you. She'd never want to miss a practice," then clearly we're not worried about you bad mouthing her.

- If your daughter wants to vent about an argument she's having with Mom, be there for her, but be neutral, and be cautious. She wants you to listen. If she wants your opinion, she'll ask. Stay neutral. She and her mom must learn to work things out without you, and in a new and effective way if you used to have the role of peacemaker in the home. Instead of being a referee, listen objectively. A response like, "Honey, you can get through this if you treat each other respectfully," or, "I can see your point. What can I do to support you with this?" might be helpful enough. Remember, your daughter wants to know you listen to her. She doesn't always want you to intervene. This is difficult for men. Generally men identify a problem and move to solution. Sometimes women don't want solutions. Sometimes we just want an ear. Understanding this about girls and women will help you get along. More about this later.

- If you have distinct concerns for her safety (is her mom drinking and driving with her in the car? Is she leaving her alone at too young an age? Is she not feeding her or maybe hitting her? Is she degrading her or eroding her self-esteem?), then listen and ask some neutral, fact-based, nonblaming questions ("How late are you home alone until?"). Tell her you hear her concerns and will consider them. Then, outside of her range, talk to trusted others. Run it past them. Seek trusted neutral people who know her so they can hear with an objective ear. Then if it seems appropriate in the best interest of her safety, consult her pediatrician, a therapist, a guidance counselor, pastor. Unless there is likelihood of danger, go legal as a last resort. If the child is in danger you must act quickly. Danger is different from discomfort.

Transition Times: Moving from Mom's House to Dad's House

Transition times happen when you and your ex trade visitation. They often happen at 4 p.m. on Sunday or Friday after school when your daughter takes the bus to your home after being with Mom for the previous days. These can tend to be, especially in the beginning, pretty fragile times for the child. She's transitioning to a different space, set of rules, level of activity or engagement, and maybe away from her group of friends or the other neighborhood's weekly Friday afternoon pick-up soccer game. It's a period of readjustment, over and over and over, more for her than you.

In our experiences, these are consistently interesting times. Just when your daughter seems to do it smoothly, a rough patch will come along. And it's likely more about something in her life that she's missing or is angry about than about you specifically. Maybe all her friends were going to talk about summer soccer camp on the bus ride home, but she's on a different bus this afternoon and feels like she'll be left out or forgotten. Maybe the boy she's crushing on lives across from her mom's house. Maybe she's missing the dog. You won't always know but you can see that she's off kilter. So what can you do to help ease transitions and help her readjust through difficult ones?

1. Don't take bumpy transitions personally. In most cases, it's really not about you, your home, or anything you've done. It's a reminder to her that her life is now different, and less simple.

   It's not uncommon for your mood to not match your daughter's mood. You're literally coming from two different places, her mom's home, and your home. You might be excited and happy to see her, and yet she is sad, distant, and withdrawn. It does not mean that she does not love you. It simply means that she's adjusting. Give her time.

   Understand that she might want to just go to her room and get settled in this space. Consider some things as you transition. Since she wasn't with you last night, you may not know that she didn't sleep much because she was at a slumber party and today she's crashing. Or that she and her mom just had an argument. Or that she is brewing a sore throat. If you are just aware of any transition patterns and needs, this will help. My daughter once said to me, "Mom, it's just that I need to settle in. I know you're glad to see me and want to start doing stuff right away, but I really need to just hang out in my room for an hour or so." I was so glad to hear her tell me what she needed, and from then on, we didn't make immediate plans for that transition time unless we talked about it on the phone the night before.

2. Tell her you understand that this is different. Tell her what you've done or will do to help this process. You only have to transition between work and home. She's got more on her plate in that sense. Let her know you're glad to see her, and give her some time. We've noticed that an hour or so really is about all that is needed for adjustment. But your daughter may need more or less. Watch her for patterns and to see how long she usually likes to ease out of one home and into another.

When a child goes from house to house, each house should be fully stocked and prepared for that child. Asking a child who is shuttling between two homes, for no fault of her own, to then make sure she is completely ready to be in the other home is an extraordinary burden, especially when rhythm of shared custody is new. Her clothes should be washed and clean and ready for her. Sometimes a simple "Why don't you unpack your backpack, settle in? Dinner's at six o'clock, or before then if you're ready" gives her the information she needs to ease in.

If she sees that she has a specific space in your home, that you are caring for her basic needs, that she does not have to come through the front door and worry about her soccer cleats or whether the jeans she left there are clean, then her transition might be eased. Many dads get a bad reputation for not taking care of daily chores, either because their domain is outside the house, or because they depended on women in their lives to do these chores.

When she knows that she can trust you to care for her needs, she can relax, which eases the transition. She doesn't really care if you bring home dinner from the Chinese place down the street or barbeque yourself; she just doesn't want be the one responsible for cooking, cleaning of the general space, like a housekeeper would. Treat her like a daughter, not a guest, not a princess, not a hired hand.

If you're to the point that she can walk in your front door, into her room, and find clothes that fit and are ready for her to wear, familiar things like photos, pillows, mementoes, then she will know that she has a place that is hers, that she is welcome, and that she is a member of your family, not a guest.

When thinking about her new space, ask if she'd like to bring some stuff from the other house to her new room, treasures she has personally chosen to bring over. You should have enough changes of clothes for the number of days she is there, plus two, even if you have ready access to a washer and dryer. Here's a basic list of things you might want to have ready for her:

- Clothes
    - Jeans, pants, shorts, skorts
    - Long- and short-sleeve tops, sweaters, sweatshirts
    - Pajamas and a robe or whatever she generally sleeps in like sweats, T-shirts, boxers
    - Underwear, socks (you can't have enough)
    - Jackets (weather appropriate)
    - Swimsuits
    - Athletic wear like soccer socks, sweats, basketball shorts if needed for her activities
- Toiletries
    - Toothbrush, floss, rubber bands if she has braces
    - Medication (a pediatrician will happily call in a second script if she understands that you need an inhaler or a bottle of cough syrup at your home)
    - Hair brush, combs, ponytail ties, headbands
    - Tampons/pads—don't panic; we'll talk about these in detail later
- Mementoes and special objects
    - Photos of her and her friends, her mom, siblings, and family
    - Familiar toys, stuffed animals, games, music
    - Books, a journal
    - Photo albums from the family
    - Things specific to your child that reflect that you know her, that she matters, and that she really does belong in this new space
- School-related stuff
    - Enough pencils and pens, paper
    - A computer if you can afford one (My ex invested in a laptop for our daughter, so it can go where she goes. Many schools have locked storage to keep these safe during the day if your child transitions during the week.)
    - Books to read

If you continue to live in the home she was raised in, you'll have it a bit easier. She has established the space already, but with a move, she may have lost some of her favorite things or left them at her mom's home. Helping her make a new space may take some money or shopping on your part but the good news is, shopping for some new things is a great bonding opportunity with your daughter. You don't have to get all new stuff—used furniture that the two of you have painted together, shopping in gently used clothing stores, watching for sales or saving up for a special object. Don't be surprised if the things that help her feel comfortable are inexpensive—a poster, some framed photos of friends, a wall calendar of frogs. If you can afford it, take her for a small, repeat *small*, shopping trip to get a few of these things. A little bit goes a long way, because the most important thing that's happening is she will get the sense that she will be a constant in your life and in that space, and that you remember that she loves frogs, the color orange, and Twilight. . . . Will it ever end?

This move might require a modicum of cooperation with her mother and hopefully she'll understand that your daughter's comfort in both homes is important. The most important mantra here is that your daughter's belongings belong to her, not to either parent. They go where she is. The child did not file the divorce papers. She should not pay the price for a failed relationship. So if she wants to take the sweater you gave her for her birthday to her mom's house, please let her. Aside from big-ticket items like furniture, a TV, a computer-based game, a piano, rugs, lamps, that sort of stuff, all her stuff should be hers. That means she gets to put it where she wants it. *Do not take it personally!* She may want to have that gift you gave her at Mom's so she can have a piece of you with her. This is a hard concept for some divorced parents to wrap their head around. After all, you're spending your money, so why should it go to her mom's house, right? Well, it goes where she would like it. What does it matter if she has a bike at your house when all her bike-riding friends are at her mom's? When we hear parents say, "I'll be damned if she brings her bike to his house," we hear, "I'll be damned if I let her be happy where she is!" To this I say, "Take a breath and for gosh sake, think of your child first!" We especially hear that about Christmas gifts and birthday gifts. Have you ever heard yourself say to a friend that you just bought a gift for, "You can use that sander on your house, but not on Dave's, because I gave it to you and I don't like Dave"? Right. That's not what giving gifts is all about and that puts your daughter in the line of fire between you and your ex. Enough said on that topic.

If you're concerned that too much clothing, books, or stuffed animals are going back to Mom's, then calmly talk about it. Ask your daughter if she has enough of what she needs at both houses. It may be that she does not have enough jeans at Mom's. Maybe she loves the jeans you got her so much that she wants to wear them Thursday to school. In a case like that, a simple "Cool. Glad you like them. I just want us to be sure you always have enough here and don't have to panic for jeans some school morning. If you take that with you, will you have enough here?" will work fine. Then she can decide what goes where. Too many parents say, "I gave you that game. It stays here." Unless you say, "Let's keep that here so we can play Scrabble each Friday," or give her a rational reason, you're really saying, "The stuff is more important than your needs."

This conversation will also give you an insight into what she's thinking about shuffling between two homes. Too often we hear daughters talking about their dad's home as her secondary home, not as important or real as the home with her mom. Although it's natural for any of us with more than one home to feel differently in both spaces, there are lots of sound reasons why daughters need to feel as welcome and at home in Dad's house. First off, if something were to happen to Mom, she should not feel like she's suddenly uprooted to your house. It should be her "other house." If she doesn't feel completely comfortable at your home, she'll want to go "home" when she's sad, sick, or troubled. This sort of relegates you to the "good-time dad" role, which is only half of being a parent. Go out of your way to help your child feel as rooted and grounded in your home as in her mother's home. It will be better for both of you in the long run. We're not recommending that you go on a shopping spree. In fact, she will be more comfortable if this space seems familiar, and that means that there are things from her history.

So if you're angry at your ex, you may need to put it behind you and share things purchased for your daughter, things like comforters, bed sheets, photos, clothes, tennis racquets, boots, stuffed animals, and more, for the sake of your daughter. The more familiar, the more comfortable she'll be. She'll realize that you respect her past and you will honor it and though her future may look different, she can rest on the foundation of her experiences, of those who love her.

A word about medications: If your child has a medical condition that requires consistent or emergency medication, ask her pediatrician to write double scripts so you have that inhaler or medicine at both homes. Don't rely on her or her mom for this. If you do, you're abdicating some of your responsibility and your own connection with important others in her life, like her doctors. By taking care of that ahead of time, you're demonstrating that you are still the responsible father you want to be. You're up to date and interested in her day-to-day health. You're showing her you're not a babysitter or a part-time parent; you're her dad. Kids watch for these signals. If you don't know the name of her coach, her doctor, and her meds, she'll see that you're not able to or don't want to go that extra mile. And whether or not that's true, trust me, she's watching for continued signs that she can rely on you when she's in a tough spot or that you care about her and know her well enough to help prevent that tough spot, like a 3 a.m. Sunday-morning asthma attack. And yes, it was easier when you were married. It's always easier having two adults handling the broad range of tasks needed to raise a healthy child. But that was then; this is now. *You can do this.*

Let's summarize a few ways to make transitions as comfortable as possible:

- Give her emotional time, each time, to transition. If she doesn't need it on any given day, she'll let you know by saying things like, "Hi, Dad, let's go get some more food for the fish now," suggesting she's in gear and ready to hang out and do things. If she needs the time, please let her have it. If she just wants to go hang out in her room (which is what girls tend to do a lot of, no matter how they feel), let her have that time. It's readjustment to space, to parenting styles and expectations; it's a pretty natural and sound regrouping style.
- Set up a room with a bed, dresser, and adequate furniture for her. She should have enough jeans, underwear, socks, shirts, sweaters, coats, and weather-appropriate stuff. If a child has to say, "I can't go sledding now. I'm at my dad's and I don't have winter boots here," then she'll not want to come to your house. If cost is an issue, ask friends for gently worn hand-me-downs. Find a local used clothing store for kids. They're every-where these days. You can, realistically, stock up on shirts and jeans and sweaters for less than $100. And then, when she outgrows them, you can resell them.
- Have spare toothbrushes, medications, and essentials so she is not responsible for remembering everything. A guest travels with their sham-poo and toothbrush. A family member does not.
- Transitions are emotional and physical. Having her "stuff" at your house will ease the physical aspect.
- Don't take difficult transitions personally. Give her time.
- When she does forget something she needs (her soccer cleats, her flute), understand she's likely doing the best she can. Parents can help with *gentle reminders to each other* ahead of time to pack the item. A child should not be punished for the very human behavior of forgetting, especially under stress. Nor should she be afraid of parents getting into

a finger-pointing fight if it requires a stop by Mom's house to get that much-needed math book.

- Remember that even when she is with you, she probably wants and needs to talk to Mom. Allow her to make phone calls when she wants. However, there is a balance, which we'll talk about later. And hopefully, Mom allows her to call you when she's with her. Remember, it's about the child knowing you're both still there for her.

- She learns about you, as a man and a father, in every interaction. If you panic when she forgets her skates at Mom's, you teach her that you can't manage or help her in a pinch. If you try to hyperarrange the transition and don't allow her to settle in, you show her that you're more concerned about you than her.

- If transitions are consistently emotionally charged (she fights with you, she becomes tearful) and you notice a pattern, then address it. When you're on an even keel and not in the middle of the mire, talk over a milkshake maybe; ask her what would help her in those moments. Tell her that you notice she is angry at you often when she first arrives, that you understand the stress and you'd like to help make it easier. Surely she'll have some ideas, if asked. It was from a moment like that that I learned that my daughter needed down time. She wanted to walk in the door, say hi, get a snack, and head to her room, settle in, and then about an hour later, she'd come down and we'd go on with the day. In letting her know she could do that, she actually needed less and less time. She became good at letting me know that she'd done her transition stuff and was now ready to head to the plant store or go to a movie or just sit and catch up.

Staying Connected When She's Not with You

Very few kids want to be only with one parent. It's not what they signed up for. They want both Mom and Dad in their lives. So you don't want to abandon her when she's with Mom, nor do you want to intrude. This is a balancing process; being present and available while respecting her time with her mom can be challenging. Just as you don't want Mom usurping your time with her, the same goes for when she's with Mom. There are several ways to stay in her life when she's with Mom.

- Send her little cards while she's at Mom's house. If you're worried she won't get them, drop them by her school.
- Set up a talk time, the same time each day so she can expect your call when it doesn't interfere with the routine at Mom's. Maybe after she gets

home from school or after dinner and before homework. Make it a "hey, what's new" light call. Don't rock her boat when she's not with you.

- In our experience, keeping the contact active while you're not together eases that house-to-house transition process. We don't have to say a big "hello" because we've never said a big "goodbye." We say, "See ya at the art show," or, "See ya at practice." And because she knows she will, her being at her dad's house is not a cut-off from Mom and vice versa.
- Use Skype for teleconferencing. Again, be respectful of her time with her mom. Don't intrude. Make it brief, happy, light. Don't start a fight or raise hard issues online or over Skype.
- Talk to her teacher and send a surprise pizza to her science class. You'll be a famously wonderful dad if you do things like that.
- Visit her at school, if that's "cool" with her. Some schools welcome parents to stop by for lunch or to take a kid for a quick lunch. If you do this, maybe she'll want a friend to come. This does not have to be expensive or fancy. A peanut butter and jelly sandwich in the car in the school parking lot talking with her means more than you think. This may call for some prearranging permission with other parents if she wants her best friend to join in the quick picnic.
- Go to practices, games, rehearsals, and shows. In real life, this means making her a priority as often as humanly possible. Not many men are supported for doing this. There is pressure to not let your personal life intrude at work. But it is important to your child. Have the necessary conversations with your boss. Set up a routine and propose it to your supervisor: I'll leave work Wednesdays at 3:30 every other week during basketball season to get to games, but I'll be in early that morning or work late on Thursday. To children, time equals importance. They will know that you have changed your world for them. There are probably other single dads in your work arena. Talk to them. Maybe you can set up a coverage schedule so you cover them during soccer season and they cover you for lacrosse.
- I make it a point not to use the phrase "I miss you" with my child when she's not with me, and here's why. I don't want her worrying about me when she's with her dad. I want her to know that I keep working, I see movies, I see friends, read books, and take care of the animals. I absolutely tell her I'm thinking of her, and don't hesitate to give her specifics like "I saw this great pair of moccasins and thought of you!" so she knows she is always with me. But if I miss her, then she might feel like she has to miss me, too. And missing suggests pining or sadness. I don't want to suggest or imply that she should be sad. So I literally say, "Thinking of you!" and she knows she's in my heart.

Contacting Mom

Here is a simple truth: daughters need their mothers. They also need their fathers. But women and men interact with their children differently. Studies show that women connect through conversation. Men connect through activity. Now we both know that there are many dads who love to sit and talk, and many moms who never stop moving. Again though, let's keep our eyes on the daughter. You will be helping her greatly if you openly give a nod to her relationship with her mom. You can show her this by making statements like, "Would you like to call your mom and talk about this? That would be okay with me if you wanted her help, too." Chances are, if you let her know that she is free to love and connect with her mom, she will get closer to you as well, feeling safe with you as you recognize that she did not divorce her mother. When you acknowledge that you understand she needs you both, she'll breathe a sigh of relief. Tell her that you know these times will come up and if you can help her get in touch with her mom, she won't have to feel like she needs to hide this from you. At the same time you can let her know through your reaction that your feelings are not hurt. And consider being proactive in situations by proposing that maybe she wants to call her mom to chat about this issue and she can use your phone if hers is dead.

She probably has some things that she wants to do with Mom, or has promised that she will do, like see a certain movie together or hike a certain mountain. If you run up against this on a Saturday morning, be flexible, offer another activity that you can do together. If she has ruled out an entire genre of activity—"I can only skate with Mom" or "I promised not to go to the movies except with her"—then you're dealing with something different. Generally kids and parents know each other's likes and dislikes, and good relationships focus on the strengths. Good parenting means not intentionally preventing bonding with the other parent or competing for the child's love and attention. If you are the type of parent who will understand that at times, your daughter will just want to talk to her mom, and that's not a commentary on her love for you, you'll find her trusting you even more. Here are some examples of things that your daughter may just want to do with Mom, and you may be just as grateful to oblige:

- Bra shopping
- Swimsuit shopping
- Makeup or skin-care-product shopping
- Stocking up on personal needs like tampons and hair-removal systems

If there is no mother available, then we'll talk later in this book about how to have a female network built up around you both, because as you know, "It takes a village. . . ."

While you're being flexible, don't underestimate how much she needs you. There is plenty of data emerging about the importance of a strong positive relationship with dad for a girl's healthy development. She learns a set of skills, love, honesty, and caring from you that is unique. You also model male behavior and decision making, which we cover in another chapter. Her mom does not always have the answer. Nor does she always have the approach your daughter wants. So when she comes to you and wants to talk, or vent about her crappy day at school, have confidence in yourself. She's coming to you for a reason.

Establishing New Traditions

When a family changes, one of the things children mourn most is the loss of traditions. No longer do you all head to the pumpkin patch to get the family pumpkins. No more visits with the whole family to Grandma and Grandpa's. Traditions are not just things that you all do together; they remind us of stability, enduring relationships, and the importance of each other. We make time, year after year, to be together and go to the lighting of the town tree. No matter what. So both as adults and children after a divorce, we miss traditions. Traditions differ from rituals, as rituals tend to be based in religious practice. The lighting of the Shabbat candles is a ritual, which can occur during the tradition of Friday-night dinner with yours and three favorite families. So traditions can be quite serious or just plain silly.

Because we often combine traditions with holidays and celebrations, the loss can be quite painful and unsettling. Rather than missing them, establish new ones! It's really not that hard. It does require some creativity, however, and laughter. When new traditions are established, they are reminders that we are still a family with the same values—especially at holidays, which are so packed with cultural and familial traditions. Establishing new ones is really essential. Traditions should reflect what you want them to. They don't have to be serious or meaningful. Their meaning may be that your life has predictable cycles. Each year at Easter we gather up the chocolate and jelly beans, park ourselves on the couch, and watch the original *Willy Wonka and the Chocolate Factory.*

If you do it together, again and again, it becomes a tradition. What starts out as a fairly easy practice can grow into a beloved multigenerational habit.

Think, for a moment, about what happy traditions you may have had grow-ing up. Often they were not extravagant. Simple, meaningful, and consistent are the hallmarks of a tradition that has legs.

Some suggestions for starting new traditions:

- Ask other families what they do for traditions. They might have some you want to steal or they will trigger thoughts of your own.
- Ask your kids. They may have some ideas of their own. Their buy-in will help. Tradition will be a sign of what's important to this new family con-stellation. Our Easter tradition clearly emphasizes the mutual dedication to dark chocolate and pectin, silly but timeless movies, and singing the same songs, citing the same lines, over and over. It's time, repetition, and predictability.
- Be open to quirky traditions. They are often the most fun. And they become unique to your family. The first year after my separation, my daughter and I talked about new traditions. She was five at the time and I wanted to see what would matter to her. Learning about the pilgrims at the time in kindergarten, my daughter suggested our new tradition, and where she came up with this I'll never know. We were to sit in a big frothy bubble bath together, eating pumpkin pie. So we did it. And we laughed. And we got some pie in the tub and some bubbles in the pie. And we realized that for several reasons, this might not be a tradition that we would be able to maintain in exactly that form. But being responsive, letting her decide on some aspect of her new Thanksgiving celebrations and being spontaneous, we made it through the first difficult Thanksgiv-ing. And it makes for a great family story.
- Consider short- and long-term traditions. Do you make blueberry pan-cakes for the hockey team the morning of a game? Do you two do the crossword puzzle together each Sunday morning?
- We also established a new holiday, with some of her friends who were also missing a parent. The holidays keep everyone moving so fast, and kids with divorced parents often are already overbooked and they miss their friends. So we established "Merry Thanksweener," a blending of Halloween (ween-er), Christmas, and Thanksgiving. The girls all dressed up in costumes and met at our house for a sleepover and bobbed for apples or whatever I had in the house, they gave each other Christmas presents (most often handmade), and ate candy. We would do something to simulate snow or sledding, sing Merry Thanksweener carols, and have

pumpkin pie. It was a precious tradition broken only when an integral member of the celebration moved away.

- Perhaps you start going to the father/daughter dinner-dance sponsored in the community, or work at a soup kitchen just before the holidays, or pick your pumpkins from the same patch each year.
- Maybe you watch the same shows together. At my house, we always watch the original version of *The Grinch Who Stole Christmas* on Christmas Eve after opening one package and getting into brand new PJs.
- When I (Gretchen) became a single mother, I realized that the Christmas season flew by, especially since I now had my daughter only 60 percent of the time. After trying to get it all in that first season, and ending up feeling stressed and sad about what we weren't able to do together, I decided to start a new tradition. Each December 1st we pick a weekday and take it off. I keep my daughter home from school, letting her teachers know ahead of time. We call it our "hookie day." We start with brunch in our favorite place and walk the main shopping street in our town. We shop for our friends, for her dad, and for some less-fortunate community family or kids. We eat whatever we want and watch the snow fly as we walk. We might then go to a movie or get our nails done. One year, we didn't plan ahead and we didn't get to take our hookie day. We both really missed it. So now, we pull out the calendar in October, pick a day, send an e-mail to the teachers, and we guarantee a dedicated hookie day. So many times the teachers respond saying, "What a great tradition! I'm going to steal it for my kids!" The fact that it's a weekday says that we matter more than work and school. Since it's less hectic in town midweek the day is low on stress and high on fun. Win-win.
- My daughter's father gives her a new charm to add to her bracelet that he started for her after we split. He chooses the charm based on something they've done and shared together that year, big or small, and he gives it to her at Christmas. Some are quite serious and some are silly, but each one is a reminder of their adventures that year.

The traditions that you will build signify passage and duration of time, stability, consistency. They will become integral to your relationship with your daughters, and sons, too. Try it out. Make some new ones; don't try to just keep the old ones going. With a mom or dad absent through divorce or death, some of the old traditions may only feel painful or empty. Some may be comforting. Don't be afraid to go new, silly, and fun. Trust me, you won't regret it.

Deployment

More and more women are both in the military and mothers. All branches of the military have deployed women to the Iraq and Afghanistan war zones. Inevitably this means that children are left behind, some with extended family members and others with fathers, who may or may not be in the military as well. When a mom is in a war zone, both the parents and children realize that in a very real way, when the mom boards the bus or plane, her children may never see her again. Death looms as a possibility, which is a completely different dynamic from the standard divorce/custody dynamic. Tweens and teens are probably more acutely aware of this possibility as they are more engaged in the larger world. Mona Pearl, both an Air Force colonel and a mother, conducted research on the effect of deployment on teenage children of deployed mothers. She found that the danger factor inherent in deployment exacerbates the stresses of being away from their parent. The longer the term of deployment, the more the negative impact on the children, which is especially important today, as more and more soldiers are experiencing multiple deployments. Not only is the waiting difficult but also the reintegration of the mom back into their lives becomes harder and harder the longer she is deployed. These risks for the teens seem to be seen in a drop in grades, poor nutritional status, and decreased exercise. These are also some symptoms of depression.

Just as the children are impacted by deployment, so are you and their mom. The recent data about the patterns of deployment are significant. Many soldiers serve one year overseas or on deployment, then a year in the states, then another year deployed. One of the most significant side effects of this pattern is found in the coping skills of the soldiers. They are trained, before going overseas, in their role of soldier, to protect and defend, to carry a weapon and to use it when and if required. Some soldiers are trained to suppress their emotions, to distance themselves as best they can from the pain and death they experience, witness, and in some cases, cause. These skills keep them alive when they are deployed, but they are not the skills that are needed in a family or as a partner. Because the military plans to redeploy the solider, they support them in maintaining the distance. The family has difficulty adjusting to Mom, and Mom has difficulty as well. Should she soften and relax into her role as mother again, or should she keep her defenses up for the intermediate months between deployments? This is a different mother and partner than you and the children are most used to, but she may be keeping her distance as a self-protective mechanism. It protects her from getting too attached since she knows she will leave again, and it frustrates and saddens the family who want her near again.

If she has been in combat or near explosions, she may have a traumatic brain injury (TBI). The TBI can cause a change in her frustration and anger response, her volatility, and her mood. TBIs are now known to cause more depression, disorientation, emotional liability, and difficulties mitigating anger. The research is only just beginning on TBI but many, many families know that they change their soldier.

While she is stationed abroad, researchers emphasize the importance of keeping the deployed mom in the loop on family life, the day to day as well as concerns, on a regular basis. This war, and future wars, will be different from previous wars. With the help of technology it's entirely possible to fire up the computer and talk face-to-face with Mom one-on-one or as a family. Sometimes partners try to protect their solider from the stresses at home and only share the best of news and not the concerns with a deployed mom. However, this leaves Mom out of her role. When deployed mothers are regularly Skyped in, they might be first to notice behavioral changes in your daughter before anyone else does. Ideally, you and your wife will have talked about this before she leaves. Does she think she can hear both the good and the challenging aspects of what is happening at home? Then, when the time comes and she is on the other side of the world, you and she know how to address the day to day at home.

As noted in an article by Ashley B. Craig in the *Charleston Daily Mail*, some military moms have become quite creative at Skyping and doing simultaneous activities with their children back home, like reading a magazine "together" in each location, looking at photos, or helping with math homework in real time. These efforts help keep the moms and teens synchronized and sharing lives, not just talking about their day. They can reference the activities in subsequent conversations. It helps put a normal flow to an abnormal situation.

Skyping with Mom is also important because research shows that fathers who remain home and caring for the teens are less likely to notice subtle changes and take longer to take them to a pediatrician for both mental and physical symptoms. Remember, moms and daughters tend to speak a more common language, so having Mom's direct interaction and observation is crucial to early detection of stress-related symptoms.

It's also important that others in your daughter's life are familiar with the stressors of having a parent deployed in a war zone. Some nonmilitary pediatricians, teachers, and therapists may not even think to look for signs of separation anxiety or stress caused by the deployment. Being a military family is an experience unique in itself. The rewards and challenges may not be clearly understood by nonmilitary families. As the parent left on the home front, your challenges are different from other single parents, because if the deployment ends, you will not remain a single parent; you'll return to the working duo with your wife.

The very fact that a deployed soldier is at risk of death in combat, and that the combat is usually reported on the news daily, adds stress and strain to the family. Look to your local military base family services office for additional information. Some bases offer adjustment groups, special social events for children and families, and readjustment support for the entire family when the solider returns. Contact the local base and see what, if anything, appeals to you and your family. Remember to keep those around you in the loop about what it's like to be a military family. Talk with your daughter about her fears about the deployment. Talking will help; it won't make her miss her mom more. She'll understand that her fears are not different from anyone else's, even yours. In doing that, she'll know that it's healthy to talk about her fears with you, with other military kids, and anyone else who really understands the stresses and strains of a military family.

If a Mother Has Died

SOME YEARS ago, a vibrant and active young mother of daughters in our community died suddenly. Erica was tall, fit, and naturally gorgeous. She was always volunteering at the elementary school her children attended. She skied in the winter, played tennis in the summer, worked out frequently, and still had time to be involved in Brownies, bottle drives, and the parent-teacher organization. To many of us, she was the mother we had always wanted to be. Her daughters were funny and adorable, and all the other kids in the school loved her. Her husband, also active and engaged, coached soccer for two of his daughters' teams. He was the CEO of a nationally known company and seemed to have the moon by the tail. Together, this family looked golden, unstoppable, and gorgeous. Erica had not been ill. Her death was immediate and completely unexpected. It's almost impossible to imagine the shock and pain that family felt.

From the moment the news of her death circulated, the community rallied around this family. Family stayed close even though neither side of their extended family lived in state. Erica's best friends rallied and supported the family, offering constant kindness, hugs and love, and memories of Mom. The children all returned to school soon after the funeral. And again, from the outside it looked like this family was back to life as usual, without Mom. Some who knew them were worried. They seemed to be moving so fast, so caught up in sports and travel and movement, we wondered how they could be grieving. Some were wondering if they might be trying hard to avoid the unavoidable, sitting with the painful absence of their beloved mom and wife.

Every weekend it seemed, they were skiing or traveling. A nanny was hired and the kids got to school, performed in plays, and the community stayed close. Several of Erica's close friends in particular kept close contact with the girls, and the aunts on both sides and both sets of grandparents were frequently seen on the soccer sidelines.

Before she died, their lives, for all intents and purposes, looked ideal. How could they keep moving so rapidly after such a loss? We wanted to reach out and say, "Stop. You cannot outrun, out-ski, out-compete, or out-travel this terrible event. Stop. Let it wash over you. It will be hard, but it will be better than this."

We all grieve differently. When a mother dies, there is no way around the pain of the loss. Regardless of whether the death is anticipated, as a result of a chronic terminal illness, or a sudden unexpected death as in this instance, grief is unavoidable. And difficult. And essential. And messy. And painful. Each type of death brings with it its own hurdles. For example, if a mother is diagnosed with breast cancer and has the disease for three years, waxing and waning while in chemo, finally dying after "putting things in order" with her husband and children, the grief will be different than the family that loses a mother in a car accident suddenly. If children witness a parent's traumatic death, the response and recovery will be profoundly more complicated and lengthy than a family who has watched a mother decline. Each death is different, and each of us is at different stages when the death occurs. Losing a mother at the age of seven is entirely different than losing a mother at twenty-seven. If you are like that dad who suddenly, or gradually, experienced the death of your wife, your grief will be different from that of your child's. You will have to take care of at least yourself if you will be of any help to your children as they grieve.

This section is by no means intended to be a comprehensive guide to helping yourself or your children grieve. We have included some other useful resources for that in the bibliography of this book. However, here are some thoughtful suggestions for you to use if you have lost your partner and are a single father trying to cope.

- Don't be afraid to let your children see you grieve. Whether or not you cry, children will feel better if they know you are feeling the loss as well. It is more reassuring to them if they see you missing their mom, crying, or in any calm way expressing emotions that they, too, are feeling. We have worked with children who really questioned whether or not their father loved their mother or missed her because they never saw him sad or cry.

- Grieving children and teens will often regress following the death of a family member or friend. They may want to sleep with the light on, bundle into the same bed with you, keep Mom's nightgown in bed with them. They will want to stay home from school at first to stay close to you. You are their remaining parent and they may not feel safe far from you. This is normal.

- However, keep school a priority. Once the funeral is over, don't keep them home from school for much more than a few days. The familiar and predictable structure, routines, sights, and sounds, along with the caring adults your children are close to are important to their slow recovery. Going to school does not mean they don't miss their mom. Some children find moments of normalcy at school, when they are back to being students, friends, soccer players. Other kids find it very hard to focus or concentrate. It is a part of normal grief to feel that you're in and out of the process, one moment a mess and crying, the next wondering if it's pizza day in the cafeteria. The child who withdraws and isolates is more at risk for complicated grief than the child who maintains relationships with peers and adults. Talk to the school staff; let them know where you can be reached if your children need you. Don't necessarily take them out of school midday if they just want to talk with you on the phone for a moment. Have regular check-ins with their teachers.

- Realize that your kids will keep an eagle-eye on you to be sure they're not going to lose you, too, and that you're functioning. So just as they go to school, they'll want to see you get up, get washed and dressed, eat some breakfast, and go to work. That doesn't mean you shouldn't say, "Today was a sad day for me, girls. I thought I saw your mom everywhere." It doesn't have to be perfect functioning; you're grieving, too. If you aren't being the parent, if they need to make you eat, or remind you to dress, they will get scared. Not only have they lost their mom, but they may wonder if they are about to lose you, too, to the grief. Talk about their mom, about what you miss, about what she means to you, about times you were frustrated or angry with her or her disease, about silly things and habits she had, even if it brings tears to your eyes and theirs. Tears are natural. Death is sad.

- Do share memories with the kids, big ones and little ones, in the moment if it seems right, like, "I remember last summer we came to this same ice cream stand and your mom ate all the cherries off the top of your sundaes!" Sharing your memories helps on many levels. It keeps them aware that you miss her, too, that she mattered to you, too (even if you were divorced or separated at the time of their mom's death). It encourages them to do the same, and reflecting on memories reminds us that we still have aspects of those we love with us. And it's a vehicle to talk about her in a way other than how she died, her disease or pain level, or other sad details. If they are not sharing their memories, encourage them to by saying, "What's your favorite Mom memory from last summer?" or some thought-stimulator. They might say they don't know and be quiet, but you've let them know you welcome talking about it with them.

- Leave much of the house the same. Some people may offer to come in and clean out Mom's closet or take her clothes to Good Will. Most kids and adults are not ready to do this soon after the death. The volunteers may not have the same feel for what's important as you and the kids do. Besides that, her absence is emptiness enough, keeping her perfume so you can sniff it, or her slippers so your kids can pad around the house in them. Save highly personal mementos to give to the kids at different stages. Jewelry, watches, certain clothes, photos, books, glasses, her favorite coffee mug. These are the things of childhood memories that also make wonderful gifts to your children over time. Let them pick out things that matter most to them in the moment. You may not know that her fleece vest is what your daughter wants most. Don't throw anything away yet. Let the kids know that there are times when you will be angry at Mom for dying (even if she couldn't help it), angry at God, and angry at the disease or the circumstance. Then let them know that most often, the anger is just a cover for the sadness.

- Give children what information they ask for. You'll know what they want to know. Answer their questions directly and simply. Don't be afraid to say, "I don't know the answer to that one, sweetie." She may want to know what you believe in as far as Heaven, death, reincarnation, the after-life, and more. Tell her what you believe.

- Actively keep important people in your lives. Reach out to your wife's best friend, as she is an important person for your kids to stay connected with. Include the school teachers, nurse, and counselors. If age appropriate, include your daughters' best friends or favorite babysitter to be a part of the team that will help you all. Keep the children connected to their mom's family, even if you aren't fond of them. Essentially, don't cut off any relationships at this point, unless they are toxic. The loss of a mom or wife is loss enough. Do expect that you will all cry, feel numb, feel angry,

feel lonely, or be in denial on any given day for years to come. Grief is a process. Loss never leaves us, we just integrate it as we go along.
- Contrary to what we have been told, there is no specific mourning period or progress through the stages of grief. They ebb and flow over time.
- The first year is the hardest. It's 365 days of "this time last year we were. . . ." It's as if we are getting daily reminders that she is not there. And it hurts. After that first year, the grief shifts and the edges smooth down just a bit. The sadness, still present, softens a bit. Don't expect much of yourself or your kids that first year. Just keep breathing.
- You will need support, too. You're watching out for your children, but who is watching out for you and how you cope? Be careful to avoid filling in the absence with alcohol, more work, or another woman. None of it works, and much of it harms you and the family. The kids need you and you need them and you all need lots of sad moments and hugging. Any filling in the blanks with alcohol, more work, or sex is temporary at best and debilitating at worst. Like it or not, feel able to or not, you really do need to be there in person and in presence for your kids.

If you are single now because your partner, wife, or lover died, your sorrows are deep and your heart has probably broken apart over and over again. You have been through so much and believe you should be strong for your children. At times it can feel like too much. If you are having any thoughts of giving up, ending your own life, this is depression, not grief. Get some help immediately. Talk to your family doctor, a clergyman, or therapist. Just talk to someone. Grief is such a long and painful process.

Unfortunately there is no way around it. If you try to avoid it, you're only postponing it. If you have children who rely on you, who are themselves grieving, then the days may be too long and you may be too scared or exhausted to do this alone.

Developmental Reactions to Death in Tweens and Teens

Grief reactions are pretty individualized, but there are enough common pieces of the process and how people react at certain stages of their life that we have a sense of how teens and tweens will react. It depends on how the death occurred, whether it was expected or unexpected, what the child saw, and developmental understandings of a life ending.

If Mom's death was violent, children may have increased fears for their own and your personal safety. If they witnessed it (a car accident, battering, murder), expect some flashbacks or nightmares. This is a feature of post-traumatic stress disorder (PTSD). We are learning more and more about how to help reduce PTSD. Consult with a therapist who is an expert in both grief and PTSD. Counseling may help all involved.

If Mom committed suicide, please get help and support from a trained therapist. Suicide leaves such wreckage for the surviving family members. It can result in increased social isolation and shame or embarrassment, overwhelming guilt that survivors didn't see it coming or couldn't change the course of events. Some people don't treat families of survivors respectfully. Case in point, only in the spring of 2011 did our president begin to send letters of condolence to families of military personnel who committed suicide while serving. Every other soldier's family has long received a letter from the president. Our government's response mirrored smaller responses in our own communities. It leaves the survivors feeling isolated and ashamed. We've heard people say, "I won't go to the funeral of someone who took their own life." Sadly, the only people impacted by this decision are the survivors, grieving family members, who desperately need to feel that their friends, family, and community are still there for them. Family members are also at higher risk of committing suicide at a later date. The anniversary dates of the death are significantly painful, as it's common to again reexamine what "we might have missed" and the guilt resumes. We strongly support you in looking for a qualified grief therapist to work with you and the children if you have experienced and suicide.

Patterns of Grief

Tweens will wonder how they will fit in if they don't have a mother. Who will go to the mother-daughter events? Who will they give their Mother's Day flower to at church? It is normal that after the loss of a parent at this age, the child reports feeling that person present. Abnormal grief at this age includes refusal to go to school, persistent depressive behaviors, drug or alcohol use, shifting away from their current friend group, and physical symptoms like lack of appetite, weight loss, and lack of sleep. Also possible is withdrawal from normal tasks.

Teens are likely to have an increased sense of care for the surviving parent. Their peers will become even more important. If those peers can't understand the enormity of this loss, they can start to isolate themselves. Abnormal grief in this group can include withdrawal from peers and group activities, increased high-risk behaviors, and a different expression of anger more akin to hostility.

In all children it is normal to see brief periods of intense grief with intermittent periods of return to normal activities and behavior. They won't always look like they are grieving. This can be problematic because those around children may see this and think that ongoing support is not needed and the child is done grieving. This is opposite of the truth. Children need continued support for the waves of grief as well as for their return to the soccer field or studies.

The school setting is so important. Children who return to the structure of their life, which is centered on school attendance, seem to do better. It is important to have teachers and counselors on the support team, as many kids will need support during the day, and their friends may as well. Quite simply, when their world turns upside down, children need routine. Please be sure to inform the teachers and guidance staff about what you have told the children regarding their mom's death, so the information can be consistent and not blindsiding the child with information that is not age appropriate or founded in rumor or misinformation.

All children—but the younger they are the more worried they will likely be—will value some reassurance that they will not now, nor will they ever, be abandoned. They may have fears for the health of the surviving parent. This is normal. Do not make false promises. The statement, "Sad and terrible things happen. Our family is in the middle of one of those times. We all love each other, and we will get through this together," repeated over and over again, in both words and actions, will help the children feel more secure.

As we mentioned, your children can cope with your crying or sadness if you always remain the adult. In fact, they may feel relieved to see you cry, because it validates that you miss their mom, too, and understand what they are feeling. However, if and when you feel the need to fall apart, try to do this with adult family, friends, or with a pastor, rabbi, or counselor. But crying in front of a child is not at all taboo. We've heard comments like, "Dad doesn't ever cry. It doesn't seem to affect him that Mom died!" Emotions are not bad. Showing your children that you can ride the waves, even the big ones, and still be okay overall, is so important for them.

Don't make the mistake of rushing to move everything out of the house that was Mom's. Don't take down photos, don't move her clothes too soon, or remove her perfume from the bathroom. If you need to clear your own space a bit, ask the children what they would like to keep in their rooms or maybe in boxes for later. Helping to keep images and memories of Mom around is healthy and helpful. If a child wishes to speak about their mom's death, or speak at a service, write about her, save or wear objects or clothes, or visit the gravesite, that's normal grieving behavior. Children generally do what they know they need. If you're not sure why your daughter is doing something or clinging to a specific item, gently ask her. "You seem to be wearing Mom's sweater all the time. I bet it smells like her a lot. Is it helping, honey?" may open the door to some information that will let you see how she is grieving. And remember to be the parent. If a neighbor or a teacher calls and says, "It's just so odd the way she won't let go of her mom's pocketbook. Can you ask her to leave it home?" please answer in support of your daughter. She is, after all, taking care of herself by keeping this with her. If the teacher is uncomfortable with her behavior, then it's the teacher's own issue, not your child's. Also, watch out for your daughter taking on the responsibilities of the family, in place of her mom. She might feel like she needs to take care of you, or no longer plays with her friends because she has to cook dinner or clean up. She is a child and needs to remain a child, doing children's tasks. She cannot take the place of her absent mother.

The mourning process is a therapeutic process, helping us integrate the loss and understand how to live on. Healthy mourning includes the freedom to express all the feelings (anger, sadness, frustration, relief, and more) related to that person and their death. Traditions are maintained as a conduit to the memories of Mom. Family members might alter the traditions (such as now taking flowers to Mom's grave on her birthday). Family and social ties are strengthened, not severed, as a result of the death. People hang on, keep caring, keep calling, and allow for children to ebb and flow through the process. Surviving parents should offer information about the death that is clear and comprehensible for their age. Children feel involved and important in decisions, including songs at a service, being present or not being present, what to wear to the funeral, how to think about Mom at the holidays and more. Children are not relegated to the sidelines of the grief. They receive reassurance that they will get through this, that Dad is still there and still the dad and, although sad, still able to love and care for them. Children are supported in having their own thoughts and feelings about the deaths. They are not marginalized.

Tweens:
The Golden Years

W HILE RIDING the escalator, I found myself behind a girl who I guessed was about eleven years old. She had a huge head of thick brown hair with unrelenting curls reaching out in all directions. She was "walking up the elevator" backward. Her black, flouncy, multilayered skirt had more volume than her hair. Under her chin was a neon-pink-and-gold scarf. Her turquoise shirt, dotted with multicolored polka dots, seemed conservative against her black-and-purple-heart-print tights and her leopard-print, sequined ballet flats. She looked like her closet had exploded and she was loving every moment of her gorgeousness. I told her she looked smashing and she confidently smiled and said, "Thanks. This outfit works for me!" That's the confidence we see at that age, and sadly that confidence can begin to erode as girls age, unless we help.

Preteens, currently known as "tweens," are in a mixed state. They are half-way between full-blown teenagers and the little girl who loves going to the dump with you on Saturday morning, followed by a bagel run and a trip to the hardware store. They are still childlike at times, and at other times emotionally all over the place. In most cases, these girls still feel like your little girl. They'll play catch with you, and they worship you. Every once in a while, however, you'll spot a cloud on the horizon, reminding you that these are special days; they will soon be emerging from their somewhat safe childhood harbors and setting out into deeper waters. But not yet. And not always.

Emotional and Physical Development

At this stage, you'll notice huge variations between girls, on all levels of growth. You might look at her soccer team and ask yourself, "Are they really all the same age?" because there is such variety in height, body type, and even maturity.

If your daughter is on either end of the spectrum, meaning she is developing rapidly or if she appears to still be quite childlike, she might wonder if she is okay, and she might be getting some negative feedback about her growth or lack of it. Remember, in a group that emphasizes sameness, and tween girls do, being an outlier can be challenging. In addition, you may notice that your daughter's behaviors, thought processes, and maturity level wax and wane. Her teachers tell you she's very bright and insightful at school, but at home she seems to be sporadic and goofy. Is she the same child? Absolutely. This is the stage of ebb and flow. She may act very mature one day, and the next not want to leave your side. She's trying to live in two worlds. She knows she's leaving childhood but may not want to be a full-time tween, and that's okay.

In this phase, she will begin to concentrate on her "self," not in an egocentric way necessarily, but in developing her own style, her own beliefs. In this phase it is inevitable that she will question your rules, your morals, and you. She'll ask, "Why," quite a bit more. If she's interested, she'll ask you about your choices in the last election, your decision to buy a new car—it's all up for exploration. And if you realize that this is not as much criticism of you but exploration of her own preferences and thinking process, you'll be less likely to answer with a knee-jerk reaction of, "Little girl, you have no right questioning adults," and instead, you'll see that these are very rich and teachable moments on decision making, ethical thought processes, and more.

At the same time, she will be more aware of who she is friends with, how she looks, whether she is popular or not, and if she is wearing the "right" jeans. Don't bother trying to understand why one navy-blue shirt is dorky now, and the other, which might look pretty much the same, is fabulous. She is responding both to the intense marketing of clothes and products toward tween girls, and to the rules of belonging that have been established in her local tween culture. This is another opportunity for some really wonderful conversations about looking deeper than the label on the back of someone's jeans, but be cautious to not initiate that in the middle of her meltdown when her in-style jeans are still wet in the dryer and she needs them for school now! Have this talk later. Please don't feel that you should cave to the pressures she feels. If you bought her a new shirt every time the styles changed, you'd essentially live at the mall in that expensive store with the incredibly loud music and the overpowering scent of their brand of cologne. But don't come down on her too hard for feeling pressures. We all do. The difference is as adults we believe that our decisions are based on wise understanding of the product. But in truth, we chose the car we did because of the image it carries. Our clothes, sports equipment, and vacation locations reflect complex pressures and image-based decisions, and what we want others to know about us. Our home does the same. She is not the only one who gets messages and feels pressure to look a certain way and have certain things. We're not saying it's right, but it is widespread and even we adults feel it. Gently remind her that there is so much more to her and her friends than the style of backpack they have. But don't be surprised if she looks at you and says, "But, Dad, you bought that new tennis racquet because it's the one we saw on TV the other day. You didn't need a new racquet, did you? And why didn't you just buy a cheaper one at Walmart? Same deal. Gets the ball over the net." She's not as much criticizing you in this case as she is reminding you of the pressures she feels that she knows, deep inside, don't make sense, but the push to be like the other girls in dress, mannerisms, and membership is there.

In situations of emotional crises like separation, divorce, remarriage of either parent, or death of a loved one, you may notice that she backslides at bit, becomes less mature or insightful. She may be becoming a bit more child-like. This is normal and should pass as adjustments are made.

Girls at this stage are not ready for total independence but they are not completely dependent either. They will start to want to impact their environment (their rooms) but they will still let that room look like a bomb exploded. They want some control (picking the color, layout) but are not so responsible that they clean it without a reminder or help. Their level of responsibility is on the rise, and the smart dad fosters this by letting them start to define it. For example, a tween may want to make a purchase of something somewhat unnecessary or extravagant. She asks for money. You say, "What would you like to do to earn that money?" In that way, you give her both responsibility and some self-determination. Sure, you don't think she needs a stuffed animal that converts into a pillow, especially one that isn't necessarily worth $25.00, but she does. So you don't fight the issue of its worth; you say, "Well, you have set a goal. I'm willing to support it by helping you earn money. What will you do to earn $25.00?" She has set a goal, made a commitment, set some outcomes, and taken on responsibility for meeting that goal. Win-win. She gets to buy her 147th stuffed animal, and you get the yard raked. She learns to take responsibility, to evaluate worth, to work for something, and to follow through with a commitment. If in a moment like this you consistently relent to her sad "I must have it, Daddy," you're missing important teachable moments. Good parenting comes when we recognize the teachable moments for what they are and we use them when they arise.

At this age, you'll get a good sense of your daughter by looking at her room. Undoubtedly you'll see clutter. She's saving mementos that you may not see the value in, but she does. If you decide to toss them without working together with her, she'll likely melt down. So leave them there. She most likely has emotional attachments to things that look trivial.

You'll notice she is becoming increasingly private. Her room is hers. Her stuff is hers. She'll probably ask you to knock on the door before entering. This is most likely not a sign of her wanting to hide things; it's a sign of her maturational process. She's not a little girl anymore, although she may seem like she still is to you. Please don't make fun of her request for privacy. She is setting her own privacy boundaries, and that's healthy. Besides, she is starting to respond to the changes her body is either making or about to make. You can even give her some positive support for setting some healthy boundaries, and add that you respect that about her, that good relationships respect boundaries (subtext: you have a right to say "there's the line;" anyone who wants more than you want to give can be kicked to the curb, and that's a good boundary).

At this stage, maintain ground rules but be ready to explain them to her. When you do this, you're teaching her some critical thinking. Show her that your rules are not arbitrary; they are based on reason and safety. "Because I said so" is a quick and easy response but doesn't teach much. "Because I'm your dad, and I'm responsible for your safety and this plan doesn't sound safe to me, so no, you can't go skiing alone without parents present" is a response that teaches. In these moments, you're showing her how to evaluate, why you came to that decision, and how to set a limit. That's an important lesson for a tween girl to learn. Even better, when you have these conversations, you'll begin to hear her thought process. "But, Dad, I don't want you there. None of the other parents stay. You'll get in our way. I'll look like the only dork with a parent present!" Whoa, skipper. Red flag. The other parents don't stay? Get in the way of what? Maybe you need to learn more about these other parents before letting her hang out with their kids.

As you're talking, she'll surely share her values with you. "Dad, we just want to feel like we're skiing on our own. I mean, we'll be doing that in three years anyway, and it's kind of fun to pretend but know you're there if we need you. You can stay in the lodge, and we'll come in and you can buy us lunch, but we just want to take the lifts on our own and not feel like babies. I think I'm responsible enough to take runs by myself. We want to talk about boys and stuff. We'll come see you. You won't be lonely in the lodge, will you?" Bingo! You have heard that she's practicing, that what she wants is some time to hang with her buddies, that she knows you'll be there and where she can find you, and that she's a pretty balanced thinker.

Both of you must feel safe as she launches. Don't confuse comfortable with safe. There will be discomfort on both parts. But if you have worked together, listening (and not always giving in), retaining boundaries, and thinking critically (not just in response to what a peer group wants), are the first steps to leaving the nest well.

By this age, children have developed and internalized values. Take every chance to hear them. It's a good time to see if what you've taught her has taken hold. Validate, validate, validate when you like what you hear. When she says, "I don't think people are being kind to Sarah at school. I let her sit with us at lunch," give her every single bit of respect and support for her decisions, her positive behaviors, her grounded thought process. Catch her "doing right" more than you catch her "doing wrong." And reward her for it with your approval and respect. It matters to her.

So what's normal and what's not for these tweens? Here's a brief list to help you get a sense of it all.

Normal Development:

- She is beginning to shift from concrete thinking to more abstract thinking. This means she's also starting to develop her own point of view. At times you may hear her pronounce her point of view about big issues, and you may want to giggle. Don't. It will hurt her feelings and you'll miss the chance to hear her tell you how her ethics and thought processes are developing. She's stretching her legs on a cognitive level. Encourage her.
- Emotionally there will be fluctuations between little kid and tween behaviors, reactions, and needs. She may have melt-downs over things that didn't bother her yesterday, like not having the "right" clothes, parties, being asked to clean her room, acne.
- She begins to worry about who she is hanging out with. Are they the "right" group? How are other girls developing physically compared to her? Because physical development at this stage varies so much, watch for and protect girls who develop physically faster. They are more vulnerable to negative comments, older boys, and maltreatment by others. Their physical maturation does not match their emotional maturation. They can be assumed to be older and approached by older peers. Parental

oversight and protection will help her not be moved emotionally faster than she is ready to.

- Friendships may, at this age, start being cliquish. This is an incredibly painful process for these girls, and seems to be at its peak in middle school, between sixth and eighth grades. The rules are cold and mean, the behaviors are cruel, and a girl can be "in" one moment and "out" the next. Do not support this behavior and watch out if your daughter is being tossed about or left on the outside.
- With the cliques will come increased peer pressure to act a certain way, dress a certain way, have certain stuff. Do not support this. Be the voice of balance. Call it what it is—inclusion or discrimination based on stuff that doesn't matter. Cliques are not based on integrity or value; they are based on superficial judgments of one person's value, based on a single aspect of their lives, rather than their value as a person.
- Physically she will put on ten to fifty-five pounds and grow two to ten inches between the ages of eight and fourteen. That's a huge and pretty rapid change, which, by its nature, generally includes a "baby fat" stage. This is just a stage and is necessary for her growth, not a sign of obesity. At this stage, parts of her may grow faster than others, so if her hands, feet, arms, and legs grow, she may be clumsy.

A Touchy Subject: Father-Daughter Physical Contact

At about this age, twelve or so, fathers begin to withhold physical affection that they may have previously lavished on their daughters. This is the same age that we begin to notice physical changes. Breast buds appear; baby fat transforms to the beginnings of curves. The problem is that for these girls, their bodies may be transitioning faster than their brains. Time after time we hear from our college students that they suddenly noticed at this age that their dad stopped hugging them, which seemed sudden, rejecting, cold, and confusing. The difficulty here is that dads are responding only to the physical changes, and withdraw, without substituting new types of physical connection. Your daughter may look like a young bikini model, but I promise you she feels like a little girl much of the time. Hugs, high fives, good night kisses, they need to continue. They need to be appropriate. Linking arms as you walk out of the movies may be comfortable for you both. It's important to develop another way to be physical that does not send a confusing sexual message. Remember, at this age she may start experiencing kisses and hugs from boys, so the physical contact between you and her needs to be parental, not sexual in any way. Perhaps this is when you start sitting on the porch steps together and just hug her when she needs it. Or the customary high/low five as you switch ends of the court in tennis. You can find a comfortable way to keep you both connected.

Here are a few more suggestions:

- Stop any touch of bottoms. This does become suggestive or sexual, even if you don't mean it to be. So no more light slaps on the butt.
- Do not make comments directed at a body part. Do not say, "Wow that shirt makes your breasts look huge!" Instead say, "A shirt with more coverage or looser fit would work better today."
- Use different language than you would use with a date. "You look hot" may be fine for your date, but not for your daughter. "You look lovely, honey. That color is great on you" works. No body parts mentioned. We know this sounds obvious but we only mention it because we've overheard really sexual remarks being tossed between fathers and daughters at times.
- Be careful to not get drawn into mixed body messages. If you get a "Dad, do these jeans make me look fat?" a great response is something like, "Honey, I'm your dad. I don't evaluate your body. Are you comfortable in the jeans? The outfit looks fine for this party." On the flip side, if she comes downstairs in a completely suggestive shirt, you should say, "That shirt is not appropriate for our dinner. Please put on something with more coverage."
- Don't comment on other girls' bodies, with the possible exception of height. Be especially careful to not comment on weight gain. However, if you see a girl who looks abnormally thin, suggesting an illness or eating disorder, you can comment and say, "She looks pale and thin. Is she okay? I can see her bones through her skin! I'd be worried about her if I were her dad."
- It's healthy to comment on ability in context. "Your arms are really stronger. Your backhand ripped right past me!"
- Girls at this stage still need and want physical contact. Hugs are okay. An arm draped over her shoulders as you walk off the basketball court, a tussle of her hair (which will no doubt bug her, but in a good way), a side body bump, or high five is fine. Yes, you do need to be alert that this can, in no way, feel or sound sexual or sexually threatening to your daughter. No, you're not a predator. Yes, you should change your behavior. Yes, she still wants your hugs and expressions of love.

Boys! (Or Maybe Girls!)

At this age girls generally do things as a peer group. So you should be aware of what her peer group is doing. If her peer group is beginning to date, you will need to start to be clear about your rules and adhere to them regardless. Again, this age group will have a wide variation in interest in dating. Some girls at this age are not interested and are focused on their sport, their studies, or just their girlfriends. Some are starting to go to movies in groups or pairs. If you wonder about your daughter, listen to everything. Listen to the conversations on the sidelines, on the drives home from the game. Listen to what the parents are noticing and what the girls and boys are saying. Again, having a strong network really helps at this point. Girls can have crushes at this age, but most don't yet want to take them any further than adoration across the cafeteria. However, if her peers are starting to spend time with boys, or girl crushes, then she will feel some pressure to do the same.

This may also be a really good time for you to begin to set your own values and expectations about dating and relationships. If she knows that you won't let her go on a solo date until she turns sixteen, then she'll know what to say if pressured. If she knows you won't let her have boys in her room, then she'll not have to wonder.

If you've never watched a movie called *Little Manhattan*, we strongly recommend you watch it. It's about first love, told through the eyes of an eleven-year-old boy, and it's a wonderful movie, and a good reminder about what it was like for all of us when we first fell in love. It's a reminder that in that moment, it's the most important love we've felt, and the most terrifying. And it should be respected. Understand that, yes, she'll fall in love again, but at this moment, her love and her pain and tears are real. If you say, "Oh honey, this is just puppy love; it will pass," then you've lost a chance. Puppy love is real and wonderful and awful, much like love in our thirties and forties and on and on. And the end of a puppy love is as painful as the end of other loves. The difference is that your daughter does not know that the pain will pass, she'll have strong feelings again, and she'll crush and love again, many times in her life.

Sexuality is emerging at this age. Crushes begin. Giggling can be heard from behind many closed doors as tweens start to feel, and discuss, those first rumblings of attraction. They are the Justin Bieber generation, attracted to nonthreatening, teeny-bopping, always-happy-all-the-time boys. Or, in some cases, girls. Adolescence is the time when most people really start be aware of who they have feelings of attraction toward and explore, then accept, then integrate their sexual identities into the people they become. For those of us who are attracted to the opposite sex, this generally comes easily.

As we know from the Kinsey report, not all of us are heterosexual, and if the first rumblings of attraction occur now, this is not exclusive to heterosexual girls. It's at this stage, as well-known developmental psychologist Erik Erikson notes, that we start identifying who we are attracted to. So, Dad, your daughter may be attracted to Justin Bieber, or she may be attracted to Selena Gomez. If she has heterosexual rumblings, she'll be in the majority, get all sorts of support for her crushes, and her daydreams and giggles can be shared openly with her friends and maybe even you. However, if she is attracted to other girls her age, or she crushes on female movie stars, singers, or actors, she might be somewhat worried about what that means for her life, her relationships with family and friends, and, in some cases, for her safety. So first, let's just acknowledge that in this stage having same-sex crushes is not uncommon and can happen to both heterosexual and homosexual tweens and teens. Both gay and straight adults can probably remember having some same-sex crushes of sorts and opposite-sex attractions.

If the tween understands that their attraction is to the same sex and that they are continuously crushing on and interested in same-sex relationships, they first come to this understanding internally. It's a process that takes time. If a person becomes clear about how consistently they are attracted to the opposite sex, that process of recognizing, expressing, and growing into a gay identity is called "coming out." Individuals generally first come out to themselves, acknowledging their own attractions, then to a close—possibly also gay—friend, and then to their families. Each of those steps presents a developmental challenge and a risk of rejection. There is fear at every new revelation. The fears are based, in general, on the levels of safety that girl has experienced. Has she heard gay jokes at home, and has Grandmother ever said, "If any of my grandchildren were gay, I'd disown them!" Has she heard a group of students call another student a fag in the hallway? What does her pastor say about gays, what does the local newspaper cover about gay or lesbian issues, and has she ever heard you and her mom make disparaging comments about gays?

Lesbian tweens and teens come in all shapes, sizes, ethnicities, and colors. Most athletes are not lesbian, and not all lesbians are athletes. Some lesbians are quite feminine and some explore the range of dress and identity from masculine to feminine. Some ride Harleys and others float about in pink tulle and toe shoes. So the most reliable way to know if your daughter is gay is to let her know that you're a safe person for her to share that with. If she thinks you'll reject her or throw her out of the house or your life, you won't be one of the people she chooses to tell.

The search for community, membership, and inclusion may take her to any local groups or agencies that respond to the gay and lesbian population.

Some schools offer Gay-Straight Alliances; many do not. Some communities sponsor tween and teen groups, such as RU12, where gay tweens and teens can meet, have socials, and work together to feel safe and included. In a sense, these groups may offer tweens and teens a safe place to land, to explore what it means to be lesbian and gay. Supportive parents are always welcome at those agencies.

Everyone realizes that just as it will take your daughter time to accept, understand, and live her sexual identity, so too it takes time for families to adjust. When we learn that someone is different from what we expected, we look to what we've lost, not what we've possibly gained.

Dad, it would be interesting if you posed the following questions to yourself in advance: What might you feel if your daughter said she was attracted to a girl rather than a boy? Would your response be supportive or rejecting? Deep down in your heart would you love her, tell her she still means the world to you, and you'll be in her corner? That's all she wants to hear, that the unconditional love she's heard about lives in your heart.

Some of the data seems to suggest that when people come out, they most fear rejection by their families (Rosario et al. 2001; Savin-Williams 1994). If we remember the importance of connection, then it becomes even more important to girl tweens that they can count on at least some of their connections continuing after they reveal this aspect of themselves. One of the resources listed at the back of the book, PFLAG (Parents and Friends of Lesbians and Gays), is a wonderful sight for moms and dads of gay or lesbian children, as well as any other friends, uncles, aunts, neighbors, and anyone interested in becoming an ally, a safe person, for that person.

"The Talk"

Yes, you have to have it. For a few reasons. You need to at least know that your daughter has an understanding of sex that is accurate, is age appropriate, and will help her make healthy decisions. You don't know that if you haven't been the one to share important information. If you have a good relationship with her mom, then you can ask if they've talked about sex. If Mom has done this, we still suggest that you reach a level of comfort that allows you to talk to her about some information, too. Most kids report that they learn about sex from peers and (gasp) TV. Unless you want your daughter to think that sex is what her best friend's big sister tells her, you've got to step up. Yes, it's daunting, and no, it's not a good enough job to buy a book and leave it on her bed. So breathe a long, deep, slow breath and remember that you have a role to play, a really important job to do.

As the most important male in her life, your take on sex (when to have it, why, and how to feel comfortable saying no) is really important. You may be the adult counterpart to her boy crush who is telling her that blue balls can kill him, and so she has to give him oral sex in the dugout. (Note: Nobody has ever died of blue balls. The simple remedy for blue balls is masturbation, and goodness knows tween and teen boys can do that!) Here are a few suggestions for how you can approach this topic:

- Don't be the voice of "Yep, it's all boys want from you, sweetie," because you know it's not true. It may be a part of what many boys want, but avoid generalizations.
- Do consider having the talk in short and frequent intervals. You don't have to have the two-hour version. You can talk topic by topic. And you don't have to wait until they are in their tweens. This can start at earlier ages when a friend's mom becomes pregnant and your daughter turns to you with questions. You may both be more comfortable that way. Don't drop the topic forever just because she says, "Dad! Yuk! I know this already!" She's embarrassed, and you're embarrassed, but remember, what she knows may be grossly off base.
- Don't let it go at "Do you know this stuff?" "Yeah Dad, we had this in school and Mom's talked to me about it." That is not your golden ticket. What you have to say about boys/men is really valuable. Share with her how mortified you were to ask a girl out, how much it hurt when that girl in science class didn't even know you were alive, and how much breakups hurt. Any shift in the tendency toward polarization (all boys want is a cheap feel, they don't care about who you are, etc.) is a good dad contribution. After all, you were a thirteen-year-old boy scared out of your wits once, too!
- Realize you both want to jump out of your skin while talking about this stuff. Don't let that put you off topic. And the more you do it, the easier it gets. Talking about it while doing something else, like cleaning a stall together or sweeping the garage, helps take the direct one-on-one pressure off.
- Do tell her your values. If you don't want her to have sex until she's in college, say that. But don't expect that's enough to mold her decision making. Tell her why you'd hope she'd wait. Tell her most of all you want her to feel completely prepared, not responsive to someone else's pressure, when making such a big decision.
- Get up to speed. Read a bit. There are trends reported among middle schools where tweens feel that anal sex is okay and expected because you

can't get pregnant and you can still say, "Yes, I've a virgin." As difficult as that may be to hear, it's out there and you should know what pressures may be on your child.

- Encourage ongoing conversations about her own values and decision making.
- Use your voice to be the voice of reason, from a male perspective. How fast should we move sexually? So many girls at this age and in high school believe that they have to have sex to "keep the guy." Why don't we teach our daughters what they expect from a guy who wants to "keep her"? In that single sentence, we are making this a two-way street, where the needs and hopes of both are important, not just the sex drive of one person.
- Get familiar with the data. Get a copy of the results of the Youth Risk Behavior Surveillance (YRBS) done every few years nationally in high school. The most recent survey was administered in 2009. In it, the data is broken down by issue (drug use, sexual activity, bullying), and read your local data. It's a good way to get beyond the myths and see what the rates of drug/alcohol and sexual involvement are among kids this age in your own community. Then talk to her about it! Since it's a report, it's a great way to start a conversation like, "Hey, honey, just saw the results of this survey. Do you think it's accurate that kids in Little City County really are having oral sex in high school?" Lean on the data to start the conversations.
- Be cautious about your language. Please do not use the word *slut*. Consider this: *slut* is a derogatory word with no parallel for males in its negativity and derision, no matter how many partners they have. You can talk about her decision making, her values, her goals for herself, and whether she knows how to say "no" without ever using the term *slut*.
- Please talk about sexual assault. Tell her she can *always* come to you, and mean it. The primary reasons why girls don't report sexual assault is out of fear they that they will be identified as "sluts" or be blamed for the assault. In many cases of sexual assault, alcohol was involved and tweens and teens are afraid to get caught drinking. In the immediate moments after an assault, one's blood alcohol content is not nearly as important in that moment as medical care and evaluation, and considerations for further safety. Blood alcohol levels of the victim are only relevant for charges that the perpetrator intentionally drugged or got her drunk as a part of the rape process. If it is proved that there was intent to intoxicate her in any way, the charges can become even more severe, especially if the victim is underage. Assault is a health crisis. She needs medical care and support, not shame and isolation. As a father, you set the tone for

being there for her in a crisis. In these situations, if a man stands up and comes forward and says, "No matter what, I love you and will help you and support you," it means more than you'll ever know. If she tells you because she feels safe with you, and you respond in a loving, caring way, then she'll likely feel more ready to tell her future partner. You've modeled behavior.

- If your daughter tells you about an assault or attempted assault, please restrain from grabbing a baseball bat and running out the door. First off, she wants you near her, not running around town looking for the guy. She needs you thinking of her, not of getting revenge. She has been violated; that's enough violence. Be her ally, her advocate, her protector, but don't be one more thing she's worried about. If anyone chases the guy, it should be a police officer. Let them do it.

- Sadly, there seems to be an increase in physical and emotional abuse in relationships as young as middle school. You, as her dad, are her protector and her role model. Learn more about the signs of emotional abuse, as that seems to be how it starts, especially in middle and high school.

- Let her know it should not come to pushing, slapping, or hitting before she asks for help. Talk to her about boys who isolate her, demean her, threaten her, and make her feel small and insignificant.

- Talk to her about cyber- and physical stalking. Talk to her about sexting and the implications of sending naked photos through cyberspace. Too often young girls hear, "I'll break up with you if you don't send me a photo or give me a blow job or have sex with me. And if you don't, I'll tell everyone you're a slut, and then you're done." Help her out way before it gets to this. Be the guy who reminds her that she never deserves this, should never expect it or think she has to do this to be loved. Remind her you will help her.

HPV Vaccine: To Vaccinate or Not to Vaccinate . . . Against Cancer

One of the most significant developments in the war against cancer, and probably one of the single most important advances in women's health and sexual health in our time, are known to the public as Gardasil or Ceravix. The human papillomavirus, specifically strains HPV16 and HPV18, is responsible for 70 percent of cervical cancers. Merck, maker of Gardasil, reports that this vaccine prevents the development of these strains at the 100-percent level. That's huge. What that means is that by being vaccinated, our daughters, and hopefully our sons, too, can breathe a lot easier when it comes to acquiring cervical cancer. There is no other vaccine, to date, that specifically helps prevent cancer. As a dad, your beliefs around this vaccine and how important it is to your daughter's health may dictate whether or not she gets the series of shots.

When the vaccine was first available, people wondered if this preventive measure would, somehow, encourage teen sexual promiscuity. Let's look at that. Tween and teen sexual behavior has not been reduced, in the past years, out of fear of sexually transmitted infection, including the chronic and often-lethal HIV. It has not been prevented by fears of pregnancy. It has not been prevented by concerns for parental respect or personal reputation. It is decreased when the tween or teen has an internal sense of herself rather than what her boyfriend wants from her. It is affected by her sense of an internal compass regarding what she wants to do, what her personal or religious beliefs are, and whether she wants to take the relationship to that level. It is affected by increasing her knowledge of sexual functioning, her body, her voice and ability to say no and hold on to her sense of self and her peer group, and, ironically, of masturbation. Fear-mongering simply does not prevent behaviors, especially among an age group that is exercising their independence from their parents, for very long.

So consider this: if there were a vaccine that we knew could significantly decrease our chances of breast cancer, prostate cancer, eye cancer, little toe cancer, most of us would get it, and we would take our children to get it. That is the case with Gardasil and Ceravix. It quite simply helps prevent, at a significant level, the likelihood that she will acquire at least one type of cancer. Where the cancer tends to develop is less the issue than being able to prevent it.

The shot comes in three doses, and all three must be administered for coverage. Parents, for the most part, play an important role in paying for and arranging for the tween or teen to get this vaccine. In a study on rates of parental compliance, 86 percent of parents interviewed were committed to the three-shot regimen (Dempsey, Singer, Clark, Davis 2009). It's important the female complete the vaccination cycle before she becomes sexually active, so some states have toyed with the idea of mandating the shot for schoolgirls starting in sixth grade.

If you have a daughter, and even a son, please consider talking to her pediatrician. The YRBS (2009) reports that the nationwide rate of sexual activity, specifically intercourse, among high school students is 34.2 percent with higher rates as they get closer to junior and senior year. Frighteningly, 39 percent of students reported being sexually active without using a condom. Even condom use does not completely protect against HPV spread. The vaccine does. Protection against cancer at this level through this vaccine is unprecedented in our healthcare arsenal. Does your daughter deserve this chance, to avoid this cancer, no matter how sexual she is at what age? We think so.

Menstruation 101: Everything You Probably Never Wanted to Hear about Periods

Okay, so you may be saying, "Do I really need to know this? Can't her mom handle this?" Nope. As long as you have your daughter with you, regardless of how often and for how many days at a time, you need this information. So we're going to talk about some stuff that might make you squirm, but you can do it.

The age of onset of menstruation these days is between nine and eleven years old, with ten as the average age. As we know, much has to change before a girl starts her period. She gains enough weight to have a fat layer that supports estrogen. She generally has started getting pubic hair and has breast growth. Her body shape changes. A waist and hips develop. She may have had some hormonal mood changes and the dreaded acne may appear. All of these are signals that she has either started or is about to start her period. So a certain level of understanding and preparation on your part is really important in helping her feel as ready as she can be.

Stocking the Bathroom

It's the scariest aisle in the supermarket and you avoid it when you can, but you know that you can't anymore. You're raising a daughter and if all is going well, she's going to need or already needs the pads and tampons that line the shelves of this no-man's land. We're talking about the "feminine product" aisle. Bursting at the seams with products that might be pretty unfamiliar to you, you've often pushed that grocery cart through it at warp speed, staring down at the shopping list, grateful that nobody ever suggested you need some man parts hygiene spray. If you had to stop to buy something for your wife or sister, you likely bought exactly the product written on the list and moved on. Now it's different. This time, you need to be the informed consumer. You, after all, are helping stock the cabinets in your daughter's bathroom with a variety of stuff. There are panty-liners, mini-pads, and maxi-pads, pads with wings and pads for nighttime, extra-long, extra-thin, and thong shaped. Moving on to tampons, do you need heavy flow, the sports models, scented, unscented, plastic applicators, paper applicators, or no applicators? What's a sane but inexperienced dad to do?

You probably shouldn't just grab a few of each and run. This won't be the last time you walk this aisle. Your daughter will need refills, and for a while, she will be more embarrassed to buy them than you're likely to be. So tag, you're it.

Breathe in, and then breathe out, nice and slow and deep. You can do this. First understand that your young daughter may be in the dark even more than you are about all these products, their differences, and how to use them. In the early months or in preparation for her period she won't be ready to jot down a shopping list for you because she won't know what she needs. It simply isn't simple, and it's confusing. The truth is, as women we have to pause, read, and figure out the symbols on the packages because the products keep changing, claiming new and improved features that claim to make our periods more manageable. Even we get confused. The differences in these products really can matter and make lives easier. So now we'll take a moment and explain in detail the differences between products so you can help your daughter and have a stocked closet. Trust us, preparation is key. No woman ever likes to be unprepared for her period. You're about to enter "The Menstrual Product Zone."

Getting Ready for the Big Day, or Night, or Afternoon. Anyway, It's Big.

We cannot stress enough how important it is to be prepared. Generally, once those physical changes we mentioned have *started*, girls will begin to menstruate about two years later. However, since menstruation is related to body fat percentage, a very thin girl may start to grow armpit hair or grow breast buds and still not be on track for menses. All girls are surprised when they finally do get their periods. No matter how prepared, it's a bit of a shock and is rarely welcomed, unless she is the last of her friends to start. Girls often feel that their bodies, now crampy, tired, bloated, and flowing, are working against them. So they get angry. It's a natural response in the beginning, wondering how much of your routine is going to be interrupted.

Even if your daughter has a mother who is actively engaged in her life, you need to know that your awareness can ease her transition. Many men are not at all comfortable with menses. Heck, in some religious traditions it's believed that menstruating women can ruin crops and sicken men. Menses have been a taboo subject for men. When I was growing up, my mom told me that I couldn't keep my box of tampons next to the toilet because it "made my older brothers uncomfortable." Needless to say, my mouth dropped open and I moved the tampons for their convenience and comfort.

Your daughter won't know how comfortable you are with menstruation unless you let her know. Drop some hints. Small ones. Not teasing hints, just toss in a "Hey, I hear dark chocolate helps cramps. Let's keep a bar around the house." Or "Wow, I remember your aunt Meg had a really tough time with her period. She used to nap for a few days because she got so tired."

Stocking up the bathroom will be one way to show her you're on the ball and care enough to support and help her, no matter how uncomfortable you are. She's uncomfortable, too. Do you remember how your mom reacted when she discovered your sheets after you started having wet dreams? If she embarrassed you, then you'll know what it's like to feel awful about a perfectly natural and really important aspect of your biological growth. If she'd said, "Hey, perfectly normal and nothing to be embarrassed about, bud. It happens to all guys. In fact, it has to happen for normal growth. What sheets do you want on the bed now?" you wouldn't have been so uncomfortable with it. This is the parallel experience for girls who are starting their periods. She, too, will have nights when she floods her pads and her sheets will need washing. It's normal, not a big deal, and nothing to be embarrassed about, except that it *is* embarrassing. So a gentle "Hey, sweetie, grab the sheets and let's get some Shout on it and not worry about it" will be a tone setter that will set the stage for communication and her relaxed response to future accidents. It's that simple. As a passing comment, toss in a quick, "Hey, kiddo, I stocked your bathroom pretty well this weekend. I'm not sure I got everything you need, but it's a start. You'll have lots of choices of pads and stuff. I got a pretty good assortment but I'm new to this too and we'll figure it out together."

So be prepared. Be overprepared. If you think your daughter has had her period but isn't telling you, you may still want to keep an eye on the amount of pads you have in the house and within easy reach at any given time. Don't make it harder on her to have to remind you, in the early months, that she is again having her period.

The Product: It's a Menstruation Jungle Out There!

Basically, the menstrual product world is divided into external protection (pads) and internal protection (tampons). As the hunter-gatherer for this expedition you'll want to know some specifics about brand, type, and absorbency.

Pads 101

Most young girls, probably every young girl, will start out using a pad. Pads are designed to sit securely in the crotch of underpants, able to directly absorb flow. They've been around for years, and thankfully have evolved into smaller, more absorbent, more comfortable items. Full-size pads now come in a variety of absorbencies, lengths, wings or no wings, and thickness. Most young girls are fearful that the pad will be so bulky that it will show through their clothes, especially shorts, gym clothes, and athletic wear. A pad can appear pretty thin and more like a panty-liner and still be used overnight because of the absorbency. Sometimes, young girls will mistakenly use panty-liners during their periods to avoid the appearance of pads. This most often is a one-time experiment, as they will inevitably end up staining their clothes or having to change their liners every fifteen minutes.

There really is no way to convince a girl that normal pads don't show, unless you can find a woman who is willing to demonstrate, by putting one on herself and putting on a similar outfit (jeans, shorts, etc.), and letting your daughter really scope out the situation from many angles.

Initially, no matter how thin, most girls say that their first experience with a pad felt like they were wearing diapers. Having anything different in her clothing is noticeable to her, as it would be to you. If you have several types, thicknesses, and shapes available for her, she'll find one she prefers. The length and shape of pads is an important feature. They match the body size and can add to comfort. Longer pads are better able to catch overflow, and pads with wings really can help keep the pad directly where it needs to be to prevent leaks. So as silly as these features sound, they have merit. Many girls like to wear longer and thicker (also called "overnight") pads during their first day or two when flow can be heavy, and at night hoping to avoid leakage. Leaks really are the most embarrassing aspect of menstruation for women and girls. They are messy and sometimes obvious and humiliating and a pain in the butt. New clothes are needed and other people may notice leaks before you do. Helping her avoid leaks is a good thing. Helping her get through it when she does have a leak is good parenting. So if she calls from school asking for another pair of jeans, please drop everything and make it so. She can't walk around school with stained clothes, which soon begin to smell and may leave stains on chairs. Kids will ridicule her. If you cannot get out of work in the event of an emergency, think ahead. Send in a spare pair of jeans that she can keep in the nurse's office or her locker or backpack.

Some pads include personal wipes in the packaging. These can make a difference for someone who is in a public bathroom stall and finds that they would like to have a little more cleaning capacity in private. They will make your daughter's life at school, camp, at the barn, or at sleepovers easier and she'll feel more confident. These little aids add up as she adjusts to life with her period and wants her privacy as well as comfort, ease, and simplicity.

Panty-liners are tiny pads not really intended for use during menstruation. They are thin, lightweight, and good for the last days of a period, but not for the first or middle days. They are used as protection "just in case." They are able to absorb the first moments of flow. They are also good at the end of a period, when flow lightens up and all but stops. Nobody wants to see her new favorite pink shorts ruined by an unexpected period. And in the beginning, before her body regulates (which can take up to a year or more) surprises are not uncommon.

If you're wondering if you need to buy both pads and liners, the answer is yes. They have different uses for different times in her cycles. She will need them both and she will love you forever for being prepared, or at least until her next mood swing hits and all bets are off.

Tampons: The Inside Story

First off, tampons are not the product that a young girl will generally want to use for the first few months, or year even, when she first gets her period. There is a lot to learn about insertion, removal, and familiarity and comfort touching one's body that, generally speaking, younger girls don't yet have. If the girl has already been sexually active, then she may have less of a hesitancy to use a tampon at a younger age. So we think that adding tampons to the mix right off the bat is not the best idea. Let's let her get used to one thing at a time.

When she is ready to start considering tampons (and often this coincides with the first summer she has her period and doesn't want to miss out on swimming), you're definitely going to need to enlist a female in helping her out. If you are a single dad with no mom in the picture, it will be important to consider who your daughter is comfortable with, as learning to insert a tampon is a highly personal experience. Perhaps a close aunt, older cousin, mother of a close friend, or caring school nurse can help. If you can't think of anyone who your daughter feels close enough to, call her pediatrician. It's likely they have a female healthcare person who is experienced in helping girls learn to use tampons. This woman should be respectful, patient, and open, and should know and like your daughter. Ask your daughter who she might feel okay with, and she might say, "Nobody, Dad, that's gross!" but really, having a woman with tampon experience at least available to talk her through it through a closed bathroom door is better than having her wing it.

The most important piece of information about tampons is that in the beginning, girls can forget that they're in, and leave them in too long, resulting in some evident odor. Girls have even inserted another tampon without removing the first because they've forgotten that it's there. That tampon can then be pushed farther into her vaginal cavity, requiring a healthcare provider to help remove it. So you see, there are more nuances to tampons than just insertion. Girls have to get used to touching themselves, knowing about absorbency, and watching out for how long they are in to avoid a serious condition called toxic shock. Toxic shock can be caused when "superabsorbent" tampons are left in overnight, or for too many hours, with heavy flow, creating a perfect environment for bacteria to grow and flourish. Toxic shock can cause death. You can, and probably should, read about it on the inside insert to any box of tampons. In general, tweens should avoid using "superabsorbent" tampons until they understand their periods and can be accountable enough to not go for too long without removing a super tampon.

Tampon use is especially helpful in reminding a girl that her life does not stop for one week a month. If she is involved in running, swimming, gymnastics, equestrian sports, or other activities that require close-fitting attire, she may not want to use a pad. If your daughter is not ready to use a tampon yet, understand and support her temporary desire to not go to the pool or not put on her riding breeches during the first few days of her period. This is really a time to not put on the "tough it out" face. Soon enough she'll realize that she doesn't want to miss out and she'll jump into her gear and go, but this takes time, familiarity with her body, and knowing how to not flood. Remember, each girl is trying to understand what is going on with her body, and what this means to her life. Answering questions from friends about why she's not going in the water or wearing her swimsuit can feel like more than she can handle at times. Support her. Offer her some reasons why she can't go swimming, like, "My dad already planned something for us that afternoon." Or let her tell the fib of "I can't swim today. I have an earache." In these moments, early on, what looks like avoidance is really regrouping and she should be supported in getting herself back on balance at her own pace. A daughter will appreciate the father who understands what's going on and helps her out.

Do Tampons Change Virgin Status?

Simply put, no. Generally, when we talk about virginity, we're speaking of a sexual status, specifically referencing vaginal penetration by a penis and whether or not a girl's hymen, a thin bit of tissue in the vagina, is still intact. Despite the years of buying goat's blood to splash on wedding-night sheets, "confirmation" that the bride was a virgin and her hymen was intact until that first glorious married moment, a hymen doesn't really mean much, and most girls, or at least most active girls, inadvertently break theirs and never know it. One good hard landing on a bike seat, a saddle, or a slippery floor is about all it takes. So a girl can have an intact hymen and use tampons or have a ruptured hymen and use tampons, but neither requires the loss of virginity. You probably already know this, but tampons and penises are not the same things! We've yet to see a penis wrapped in a pretty pink wrapper or flushed one down a toilet, but there's a first time for everything.

Most young girls really feel much more comfortable, due to the size of their pelvis, with slender tampons. They are smaller in width and easier to insert. They are smaller and will be less formidable looking to your young daughter. Just check out the label and look for *slender*.

Direct-Contact versus Insertion-Guide Tampons

As much as the environment is on all of our minds, we would suggest that until your daughter gets used to using tampons, she'll likely find the brands with either plastic or paper insertion guides far more comfortable to use. First of all, these guides are usually textured and shaped to ease insertion. That's key. Next, if the guide does all the work, nobody ends up with stained hands in a middle school stall, trying to figure out how to get to the sink without someone thinking you've committed a murder in there. Finally, most young girls are not that comfortable having the direct labial contact required by direct-insertion (meaning no-guide) tampons. Some adult women never get comfortable enough touching themselves to master the direct-contact type. So get ones with guides.

Sports Tampons?

What are these, you may wonder. Do they help you hit the ball back over the net harder? Do you jump higher? Run faster? In an interesting way, yes, they might. Sports tampons looked like yet another marketing gimmick when they came out, but upon close examination and customer-satisfaction comments, along with actual case studies by our friends, these tampons do seem to expand differently once inserted, in a way that prevents leakage while a body is flinging itself across a track or a softball field going for that pop fly. And remember, keeping your daughter feeling more like herself than not, helping her keep her activity level up, and increasing her confidence that she can do all the things she wants to do even with her period will help her continue to grow and not feel left out of the fun for one week a month. To date, none of these sports tampons have team logos on them, but it's only a matter of time before someone figures out how to support the U.S. women's ice hockey team or the Olympic women's water polo team by purchasing their logo'd tampons. As long as they don't leak inks or dyes into a vagina, we're cool with that.

A Word about Toxic Shock

Unlike sticker shock, toxic shock really can kill you. It's a type of bacterial infection that can occur in many places but flourishes in dark, warm areas where there are lots of nutrients. And that describes a menstruating vagina. The use of superabsorbency tampons is generally not encouraged, as it allows for the conditions to remain perfect for a longer amount of time. More dark, more warm, more nutrients. Changing tampons can save a life. If a tampon is so absorbent that it doesn't need frequent changing, a girl can pay a high price if she goes ten hours without changing it. They simply are not a good choice for girls less familiar with having their period. Don't feel embarrassed to talk about toxic shock with your daughter. Someone needs to.

Fun with Tampons

Yes, you should probably buy stock in tampons. You most certainly will spend a lot of money on them, month after month for years. They will add more to your daughter's life than they will take from your wallet. For many girls, tampons are a pretty new and daunting concept, especially if there is no mom or older sister around. Comfort only comes with familiarity. We encourage you to be willing to waste a box or two by encouraging your daughter and her friends to pull them apart, experiment with them in the bathroom sink, check out their appearance, "launch mechanisms," and feel. One friend related a wonderful story in which her daughter, thinking about trying out tampons for the first time, sat in the bathroom with a friend for over an hour, launching tampons like rockets across the room into the tub for points. That was a well-spent $4.79. The mystery of the great white tampon was erased, their absorbency was put to the test, and the edge was taken off with raucous laughter. In fact, Dad, it may not be a bad idea for you to take a few tampons out, read the directions that come in every packet, and get to know a bit about the product. And maybe launch a few yourself.

What's Up with Organic Tampons?

Concern has been expressed that nonorganic tampons have been bleached and may, due to manufacturing processes, have been exposed to fibers and chemicals that when inserted into a human body could be a health risk. As far as we could find in a data search, the organic versus mass-production tampons debate continues. This debate will continue, and there are, as of this printing, no clear scientific data suggesting that mass-produced tampons used as directed are harmful. The jury remains out and the conversation and research will continue.

A Word about Scented Tampons, Scented Pads, Douches, and Feminine Hygiene Sprays

Women do not need, nor should they use, scented products vaginally. And here's why: our groins are loaded with sweat glands. Both men and women have specific scent signatures that are meant to attract one another on a very primitive level. It's called *musk*, and it attracts us to one another as possible mating partners. Our scents are there, and have been for thousands of years, for a biological reason. Thank goodness we shower more than our caveman cousins, so we don't smell like they did. We use colognes and scents to attract others. But our natural scent remains. Since our groins are loaded with those scent glands, making that smell "unattractive" or something bad is not such a good idea.

Using scented products can cause allergic reactions and tissue irritation in very sensitive areas. This skin is not like the skin on our arms, where we can easily slap any old scented lotion on with little or no feeling or reaction. If you doubt that, get yourself into the shower and lather up the old privates with harsh soaps, heavily scented soaps, and other products like tea-tree shampoo. You'll see what we mean. The scents may well irritate and inflame tissue. No thank you.

Next, suggesting that a girl's normal smell is offensive is, well, offensive. Across her menstrual cycle, a girl's scent, and her vaginal discharge, will and should change. It's important that she knows that the scents and discharges are normal, natural, and healthy. If she is comfortable with her normal scents, she will also be able to recognize if the scent changes or the discharge takes on a different color and either could indicate a bacterial, viral, or parasitic issue, which should be checked out ASAP. If she covers that scent with a perfumed pad or spray, she might be missing the clues that there is something going on that needs medical attention.

Pads are made to absorb. If we use them for too many hours without changing them, they will start to develop an unpleasant smell. This smell provides a teachable moment, telling the girl, "Hey, you went too long before heading to the bathroom." In this case, smell teaches hygiene. It doesn't take many of these moments for the girl to learn more about how often to attend to her period. If the pad is scented, she's missing the learning.

Finally, if that doesn't convince you to not buy these products, let me tell you a little story a nurse friend shared. As a rural nurse in New England she made many home visits. One day, a woman asked her why she was so itchy and sensitive "down there." Upon examination, this nurse found that the woman's crotch was the color of a four-alarm fire and just as burned. When she asked the woman what sort of laundry detergent she was using, the woman responded, "The only thing I use is Pine Sol. I douche with it a couple times a week. Have all my life. I want to keep myself clean and smelling nice for my man." Besides the fact that this nurse then knew that this woman's man was a woodsman who liked the chemical smell of a pretty hardcore household cleaner, the nurse realized that this woman has been doing damage to her tender parts out of ignorance and concern that she naturally smelled offensive. Don't do anything to suggest to your daughter that her natural scent is offensive. We don't need to smell like a lilac bush or a cool summer breeze. We just need to smell healthy.

A Handy Dandy Premenstrual Shopping List for Stocking the Bathroom

- Panty-liners:
  - 1 package of longs
  - 1 package of extra-thins
  - 1 package with wings
- Pads:
  - 2 packages of long, thin, overnight absorbencies with wings (you should be able to find a brand that combines all three features)
  - 2 packages of regulars (not overnights) with wings
- Tampons:
  - 1 package of slender, regular absorbency with applicators
  - 1 package of sport tampons with applicators
    (*Note*: At the time this book was printed, the only nonapplicator brand we were familiar with was the OB brand of tampons. All others have applicators unless specified otherwise. Your daughter may try them later, and prefer them, but at first an applicator eases the transition to insertion.)

- 1 small tube of KY Jelly or a non-scented hypoallergenic lotion, cream, or jelly for those first few insertion efforts.
- Over-the-counter pain medications. Naproxen sodium has an added benefit of both helping to relieve cramps, muscle aches, and pains, and lessening menstrual flow. Some girls swear by the menstrual pain relievers, which are also reported to help with bloating along with cramps, headaches, and joint and muscle aches.
- 1 heating pad—always good to have around, and they really do help with cramps.
- Extra pairs of comfortable underwear. Leaks, which happen much more in the early years, mean a greater need for more panties. So unless you want to be doing extra loads of laundry, have more than enough in the house. Some girls also want to hide a spare pair in their gym lockers, the nurse's office, their backpack, or tack box, which is not a bad idea at all. Put them in a small zipped plastic bag for her, along with extra pads and tampons, and let her leave them, like a squirrel stashes nuts in the fall, anywhere she feels she needs them.
- Chocolate—some girls really do crave chocolate. Get the good stuff. She'll love you for it.
- Tea—a warm cup of tea can help with cramps, too. There are some brands of tea that state they specifically help during menstruation.
- Salty stuff—like chocolate, some girls crave salt when they have their period. The optimal "cover all the bases menstrual snack extravaganza" just may be chocolate-covered pretzels with a side serving of ice cream. The dad who makes that for his menstrual missy is going to go down in dad history, trust us.

Well, we really appreciate you hanging in for that! That was a lot of menstrual nuts and bolts, but we hope you know far more about what your daughter will go through and what you need to have and do to help her than you ever thought you wanted to know. If you know this stuff, she will really appreciate that you cared enough about her body, her growth, and her changes to get up to speed.

Tween Friendships

The key points to remember are that your daughter is seeking connection and belonging with friends. During the tween time of life, friendships are likely still a result of connections with sports and with families. Chances are that your daughter has some friendship with the daughter of either your close friends or her mom's friends. In fact, some parents also urge their daughters to be best friends, as if to validate the adult friendship. This can be especially acute with mothers who can superimpose the strength of their own relationships with the strength of their daughters' relationships. It's entirely possible that two daughters will not click despite the strength of their moms' friendship. Some tweens feel stressed when they find they don't really like their mom's best friend's daughters. If you notice your daughter is in this dilemma, support her in being kind to that girl, but remind her that her friends are her own, and she can choose them wisely. Not everyone clicks well enough to be a close friend, but we can have many levels of friends and maybe there is room for this girl somewhere in her world or maybe there isn't. She does not need to be a friend with this girl if there is no click, no common ground other than their mothers.

Tweens have strong best-friend attachments. What differs between tweens and teens is that best friends can be really strong one day and dissolve the next. So there can be a long-term best friend or a revolving door with frequent best-friend changes. This does not necessarily represent a problem in maintaining friendships; it more likely reflects common interests. As interests or teams shift, so do friendships. What it can mean is a little heartbreak. If your daughter's best friend moves on because she has met someone else who now plays lacrosse, your daughter may well feel left behind and as if she is not good enough. This is an important moment to remind your saddened daughter that all relationships have an element of fit, and at her age, when so much change happens, it's challenging to keep the fit. Growth brings change, which can bring sadness. Remind her that she, too, will likely find herself growing past a certain friendship. The heartbreaks generally come when the girl who moves on insinuates some sense of blame on the friend left behind, as in the case of someone saying, "I can't be your best friend anymore because you don't date yet, so we have nothing in common." Ouch. That's especially hurtful when it involves different maturity levels. Inevitably, the less mature girl thinks that she's just a "baby" or "not cool enough." And this can hurt. Girls will not hesitate to let the other know that they dress like little girls, or they don't understand what it's like to have a crush, or they are growing up faster than their friend physically. Remember that at this stage, you may just as easily watch your daughter move from tomboy to scientist to political essayist and back to that girl who takes out her trunk full of American Girl Dolls to reorganize their clothes. She feels caught between ages and is comfortable with being in both. And some friendships will demand that she pick a spot and leave the rest behind.

Generally these friendships are based on fun and games. Literally. That's why team sports or joint ventures, summer-camp friendships, and church groups can be such a wealth of potential friends at this age. The tweens come together under a common banner and can then find their new friends in the fine lines. These girls are not as interested in being popular in the larger tween community if they have their good, solid tween friendships. And these girls are still very interested in pleasing the adults around them. So car washes, bottle drives, clean-up days, and raising money for a cause really draw their attention. They get to have fun and to please adults.

This is also the age when it becomes clear that overscheduling can take a toll on the entire home. Yes, adults have work commitments that require them to have afterschool care, but please be careful to reserve downtime for your tween daughter. Just like you, she really does need to learn to balance her life, with the right amount of studying, organized play, and relaxation. As Americans we have come to confuse relaxation with doing. We relax by running, working out, moving. There is a need, a real need in our overscheduled immediate gratification culture, to be able to take a book and just read, to be able to thumb casually through a magazine, to pull out a sketch pad and doodle, or sit and knit. There is value in quiet. Encourage your daughter at this age to enjoy those moments. As she feels a little scattered and movement-oriented, the ability to pause without a goal is a real skill that will be useful for her across her lifespan. If you are good at this type of relaxation, show her how to do this. Hang out in the yard in the hammock with her; let her see you quietly on the couch with a new magazine.

As her dad, you can be a real support for her at this stage by supporting her friendships. Open your home to sleepovers or spontaneous Saturday-afternoon gatherings; include her friends by being flexible. Don't be afraid of last-minute "Hey, Dad, can I call Mattie and ask if she can come with us to the beach tomorrow?" invitations. Prepare for the giggling. There will be giggling and silliness that can seem to roll well past the norm. You can easily end up on a two-hour ride to the beach with a few girls who are starting to grate on your nerves with their voice pitch and their giggling. Take a breath, turn up the radio, drink some water, and remember that you are helping make a memory of a great day. Model being a good friend by letting her get a glimpse of your friendships. If you can, socialize with other families so your children can watch other adults and can observe a range of communication skills and ways to show caring. And no matter how much your heart aches if she is sad due to a friendship shift or change, be there to support and listen to her, but don't intervene too quickly.

Some girls have huge groups of friends and others a few select friends. Neither approach is better than the other and both come with downsides. She'll find a way that feels best to her. At the same time, while she wants to be connected and belong, cliques are on the rise. By nature, groups are not inherently bad. It's the accepted behaviors of that group that can be disquieting. In girl cliques, members are either in and on good standing, or out and being ignored, ostracized, or worse, bullied. Keep an ear to the ground for these behaviors, and for your daughter's behaviors. It's possible that our daughters are being bullied, and at the same time, it's possible that our daughters are the bullies. Be aware of the potential for both. If another parent, teacher, youth group leader, or child mentions that your daughter is behaving in a mean way, don't brush it aside.

At the same age, girls move from group to group. They may be in a group for the duration of a sports season, or while the play is going on. But generally, she will have some overlapping or lingering friendships regardless of the time of year. Help her keep herself exposed to a broad net of friendships so when some fall apart, there are others still intact. This stage does not last too long, and soon enough you'll be looking back on it and relishing its easiness. It does seem less complicated, simpler, and more fun-loving. Yes there may be some drama, but all in all, enjoy this stage. For some girls, it's the calm before the storm.

The Teen Years
. . . Whatever!

I T'S IRONIC that the job of a parent in this stage is to nurture and raise these children as they move closer and closer to the edge of the nest as they prepare to launch. We trust them to use the skills we've taught them, to fly. So why is it that during their teen years (ages thirteen to eighteen) it feels as if our trust is tested over and over? We know it's fact that their brains won't be mature until they are about twenty-two years old. We also know that they need to test their wings. They need to disagree with our politics, tell us we're crazy to vote for that candidate, remind us we're dinosaurs because we don't know the difference between and an iPad and a legal pad. For every small epiphany, they are learning more about who they are than who we aren't. And that's the work of this age. The problems for parents come when we try to keep teens from growing. We might as well try to fold their bodies into a pretzel and load them into a stroller for a walk as expect them to respond to us and life like they did in the peaceful preadolescent years. And Dad, there's the rub. We have to help them differentiate, and let them move away from us, because if we do this and do it well, they won't go far. They won't summarily reject us. They'll be back, but only if we let them go. Ironic, no? Painful, yes. Scary, definitely.

As a culture, Americans expect that the teen years will be a small, or possibly big, slice of hell. We expect our children will push us at every turn, that they are out of control and will only come back to us when their hormones have stabilized. We expect major rifts in our relationships, late nights spent in fear waiting for the phone to ring, and in many cases, a trip or two to the local jail to bail them out for something or other. We seem to think that rebellion and differentiation are the same thing, and that it must happen with a strong overtone of disrespect and chaos. How we ever got to this point, we'll never know. But I do know that friends of mine from other cultures do not expect such catastrophic experiences from adolescence.

Maybe we can mitigate the level of chaos that might come with this age. Maybe if we understand it and expect different, we just might have a different experience. So first let's look at the physical and emotional tasks that teen girls face.

What's Going On in That Head of Hers?

The emotional task of adolescence is the same for parents as it is for kids. We are in the process of letting one another go, or more realistically, letting the relationship we have had for so long change. For kids this is challenging and many of them have moments of abject fear. They are looking at increased responsibility on more levels as some begin to pay for their own clothes, car insurance, movies. They are joining in and behaving responsibly with their boy and girl friends, establishing and managing—even if it's briefly—the rhythms of a more grown-up relationship. They are differentiating from us, learning what they like, believe in, will support, and don't want to be. Sometimes they don't want to be us, at least not until they can get some distance to see if they want the same landscape we have planted for ourselves. This differentiation process is challenging for everyone. If you don't think your kiddo is scared to death about not being your "little girl" any longer, you couldn't be more wrong. And if you think you're not scared that she won't like and respect the adult you are, and that you'll lose her, you're equally wrong. We're all scared.

A teen girl is a little like a frog in a whirlpool. They're all over the place and don't know when the swirling will stop. Their physiological changes, which started in years ago, around the age of eight, continue, and some of those changes are quite daunting for parents to understand, much less watch. Please remember that just because your daughter's body has started to mature, as far as primary and secondary sexual development is concerned, her brain may not be in the same place. She is not necessarily the girl on the inside that matches the young woman on the outside. According to Dr. Louann Brizendine, author of *The Female Brain*, during puberty, a girl's entire biological reason for being is to become sexually desirable and attract mates.

Okay Dad, breathe. Slowly inhale; slowly exhale. That's her biological imperative. It gets complicated because she is no longer just a set of bones and muscle competing for sexual mates; she is also growing emotionally and intellectually. But make no mistake, she is deeply affected by her hormones, which have still not stabilized. These hormonal shifts affect not only her sex drive but also her behaviors. Puberty is a stressful time and because of the hormonal shifts, girls are easily stressed. Let's understand the menstrual cycle just a little more deeply. During the first two weeks, estrogen surges and this triggers a need for connection and social interest. The third and fourth week bring an increase in progesterone, which causes an increase in irritability and an interest in being left alone. So the cycles of behavior, getting close and then seeking refuge in her room, are hormonally driven. Estrogen activates oxytocin, the bonding hormone that is also released during breastfeeding and at orgasm, which causes increased desire for talking, connection, flirting, and socializing. The more intimacy a person is having, the more oxytocin floods their system. It is both the cause and effect of intimacy. With teen girls, the drive for intimacy meets the drive for impulsivity, also caused by the brain.

In comparison, teen boys are largely affected by testosterone, a hormone that seems to actually decrease the desire for intimacy and increase an interest in conflict, competition, and being the top man on the totem pole. As you can see, this is almost exactly opposite the hormonal drives in girls. Girls are seeking connection, and boys are seeking conflict and competition. This is likely the reason why girls tend to fall in love and boys tend to talk in the locker room about the girls who love them. It establishes their location in the hierarchy. Teen boys spend 65 percent of their free time in competitive games while girls spend 35 percent (Brizendine 2010). More and more the research shows that brains are not mature until the early twenties. Hormones alone don't cause the behavior, but they do drive us and enhance impulsivity.

Girls are more tuned to voice and slight changes in facial expression. To some, especially males who aren't familiar with this, it looks like increased sensitivity. However, because women are drawn to connection, with this ability to register inclusion or exclusion at the earliest possible moment, they are more likely to be able to maintain social and loving connections. Because of this drive for connection, teen girls are highly susceptible to "fitting in" to a group in any manner possible, in clothing style, language, music. Teen magazines are directed at teaching teen girls to behave like one large mass of teen girl sameness. Remember when she started playing soccer in kindergarten? Friends used to call that "Amoeba Ball" because the whole mass of little girls would circle around the ball, no outliers, not backfield waiting for a pass, just one large blob of little purple T-shirts. Well, on an emotional level this is not much different. Connection is key.

For parents, this can be exasperating. We want our daughters to think for themselves, act on their own, use their own heads. They will, in steps, sometimes in quiet or in the comfort of one-on-one friendships, or in the privacy of their own rooms. You might hear bits and pieces as you talk about things while driving home from the game with her. Trust her. She's emerging. Support her when you hear it, and don't reject her when she is one of the crowd.

Finally, please realize parents really can't help but embarrass our teenage daughters. All the time. Everywhere. When we ask strangers for directions. When we dance a bit in the grocery. When we sing along to songs. When we drop them off at school and the windows are down and kids can hear our music. When we shop with them, walk with them, and almost always. We believe it is a parent's God-given right to embarrass our teens. The embarrassment stems from belonging. We are doing things that, they perceive, could jeopardize their belonging to groups. If their friends love that we sing in the car with the windows down, our daughters will suddenly find this less embarrassing and just quirky. We need to breathe, to remember that we are good parents and that this embarrassment thing is more about them than us. You may notice that boys are generally less embarrassed. It goes back again to the drive women feel to connect.

Teens and Friendships

A study by the Kaiser Family Foundation (1999) found that between the ages of thirteen and fifteen, the spheres of influence for our children shift away from family to the larger outside world. In this age group 64 percent of teens said their friends were most important, and 61 percent reported that TV was an important source of information and influence, followed next by teachers, and then the Internet. Parents came in at a whopping 38 percent. So there you have it. Hard data that lets us know what we assumed. But should we, as parents, accept that we are less influential than the Internet? We would suggest not, but that we need to do parenting slightly differently and understand the changes inherent in this age group.

At this age, friends are increasingly important sources of information, support, translation, and indoctrination. It's important when hearing the data from this to remember that not all peer influence is negative. If our daughters have good solid friends, then they will be safer. However, you are less likely to know these friends as well as you knew her middle school and elementary school friends. You may not even know their parents or, in fact, know all of the friends she has. This is where we put in the plug to remember your networking. Although high school generally requires less involvement by parents—more and more information is sent out in vague newsletters from the teachers or administration—stay in direct contact with teachers, coaches, and other parents. Be there to drive to and from dances and events. The better your ability to listen to what you hear on car rides and as you pop the popcorn for sleepovers, the greater your understanding of who your daughter is friends with.

At this stage, friendships are quite different from tween friendships. Developmentally, this may be the first time when she picks her friends largely independent of us. These friendships are not forged out of play dates or teams or made because their moms are best friends and the kids are friends because they're spending time together. These are friendships made over the chemistry lab table, on field trips, or through other commonalities that can be a mystery at first glance to parents. This is the first real stage when a girl's friendships are more likely reflections of themselves. She has chosen this person for a reason. Something about that person intrigues and engages her but we may not know or understand what this attraction is. At this point, our daughters may connect with someone who seems completely different from her. If you cannot see the connection, breathe and pause, and then gently ask about what attracts her to this new friend. Appearance is one of the avenues that teens use to differentiate from their parents. It's the most effective way to very quickly establish "I'm not my mom" when her hair is green and she's wearing cat's-eye glasses. For whatever reason, your daughter is attracted to some feature of this person. Lots of kids with green hair love chess, volunteer at the humane society, or love the same authors your daughter does. If, in a quiet moment, you ask your daughter about that connection, she just might tell you. If you start off with "Where did you meet her?" she might feel slightly interrogated. Begin with questions like, "You're really good at reading people. What did you see in Ellie that caught your interest?" The more neutral the approach, the more likely you are to hear what matters. The less she feels like she has to defend her friends, and the way she selects friends, the more comfortable she'll be giving you some insight. Remember that even as they are growing up and seemingly "away" from us, they continue to be, at their core, more like us than not. Their moral principles, their values, their beliefs tend to remain close to how we raised them. This doesn't mean they won't go through a stage of reexamining them, but overall, they stay consistent. If we were to sit in on a high school history class, as flies on the wall, and listened to our daughters discuss their voting preferences, we'd likely hear some of our beliefs in their words. So, too, with what they value in people.

Your experience of teen friendships, as a guy, was likely completely different from your daughter's. Boys have larger friendship groups, with far less verbal intimacy. They are based far more on common activities and much less on vulnerability. Boys are comfortable "besting" one another to establish and reestablish rank orders in friendship groups. This is accepted behavior and generally boys don't take it personally. If one guy has more touchdowns than the other, he's more valued on the team. No hard feelings, just fact. Rank is established and maintained in a pretty data-driven way. The way to move past him in rank is to outscore him. It's not personal; it's acceptable. Male friendships are less volatile, have less drama. Where activity is the key to male teen relationships, intimacy and vulnerability is key to girls' relationships. So no doubt you will, as a dad, shake your head and wonder why it has to be so difficult and volatile for your daughter. It may also be easier, for these reasons, for you to stand back and see the ups and downs of a teen girl's relationship as far more complex than they need to be. You have valuable insights and perspectives, but they will only be welcomed by your daughter if she comes to you, for the most part, to get them. If she asks, be honest. Share your observations. She may well agree with you, or learn a new perspective. Also, be aware that your responses to your daughter's friendship issues might be significantly different from her mom's. Her mom was once in this dance and may well be triggered by hearing that her daughter is going through similar situations that were painful for her as a teen. Your bit of objectivity and distance can be a welcomed anecdote if Mom is overinvolved in her daughter's friendships.

At a time when our daughters are getting ready to launch, they are also moving away from us in their friendships. They will tend to talk more intimately about their day-to-day experiences, their worries, their crushes with their friends rather than with their parents. As parents, we can begin to feel like we matter less. We hear less and less of her personal life. She likely spends more time on the phone with her friends, more time on weekends with her friends, and you may feel shoved aside. As difficult as this can be, she still needs you and wants you there. Don't take it personally when you feel like you're on the outer circle. You still matter a great deal.

Because the content of what they share with their close friends is more and more personal, the intensity of those relationships also increases. Girls become very vulnerable with one another, and as they do, they share more and more intimate thoughts and details about their lives, ambitions, and loves. This can make for some increased turmoil and volatility between friends. The friendships matter deeply; the content is highly personal. One day a friend can be stapled to their sides and the next day they are not speaking and your daughter may be an emotional mess. She has divulged a great deal to someone who she is not speaking to. This confuses her and scares her. This person has the ability to really hurt her, make her secrets known to others, and the ensuing hours or days can be quite turbulent. Almost overnight, a best friend can become an ex-friend. And then twenty-four hours later, they are again best friends. Remember that the basis of female relationships is connection. The breach in a connection can be scary, and how each girl handles it tells us a bit about their level of empathy and integrity. At this juncture, we can gently remind them that no matter what the outcome of the relationship, others will view them in terms of how they handle the rift. If they start to share the deepest secrets their best friend shared in trust, then someone will likely do the same to them. Handling this conflict well will really help her learn a conflict-management skill. She does not have to demoralize someone who meant a great deal to her as a part of ending a friendship (or later, a love relationship).

Friendships with boys are more common among middle school kids, but in some cases, they extend on in life. It's not easy to maintain male/female friendships in high school, but it's possible. These are quite valuable relationships, because they give both kids a chance to hear from the other sex, learning from the inside-out about the differences and similarities. One sure way to squash this relationship is to tease your daughter about it. If she feels as if her relationship can only be seen as a pre-dating situation, or it can't possibly be "just a friendship," it will support a strain on the relationship. Having a really solid guy as a good friend is an advantage on many levels to your daughter. You can support it by dropping quick but clear messages like, "I like Dave. I'm glad he's your friend." Her friendship is validated and supported. In general, be supportive of her commitment to her friends, her ability to establish and maintain friends, her willingness to forgive friends who are not perfect, and her ability to have a broad range of friends.

So what do you do, as she's angry and crying and on the phone with her other friends, bouncing to the rhythms of an emotional run-and-gun basketball game? You sit, and wait, and let her know you're there, and you get that she's in a friendship crisis if she wants to talk. This may not be easy, because where you once felt pushed out of her inner circle, you may now see an opening. But sit quietly, let her know you're there, and if she needs you, she'll come to talk to you, or just ask for a hug.

Dating

By the time she's a teen, your daughter will likely have had some crushes and possibly some early relationships. She may be attracted to boys, girls, or both. She may be very much on the dating scene or be more focused on her studies and sports. Regardless of what she's doing, she's likely increasingly aware of a drive to experience a relationship of some sort. It is not uncommon for the girls who are dating to be seen by her peer group as more successful over all, and those who are not dating can be viewed as losers or worse. So at times, her dating status can mean more than what she is doing this Friday. For a girl who looks for external validation, this is a difficult and painful truth. If she is not chased after, then maybe she is not worth chasing. Sadly, dating gives her status, even if she is not interested or ready. Who she dances with at the school social, who meets her at her locker, and what status she posts on Facebook are all public flag flying. Just as being the captain of the lacrosse team signals a boy's rank, who she dates signals a girl's rank and value. This is even more powerful if she is running in a group where dating is valued. If her friendship group is not yet dating, they at least provide her with a sense of camaraderie, similarity, and safety.

As your daughter's interest in dating grows, undoubtedly your buttons will be pushed. We simply never seem ready for our children to take that step of dating. It reminds us of our own teen experiences with love and lust, both good and painful. It reminds us that although we are raising her to leave the nest successfully and ready to soar, seeing her get in a car with a guy just really makes it real that she will, indeed, leave us. So this is the point, or before this if you can, where you might really want to pause for a moment and examine your own fears so you don't forward them on to your children. There is a broad range of experiences when dating. What we experienced will not necessarily be similar to our daughters' experiences. And we need to make room for that. They are, as we were, expecting and looking for more freedom as they grow up. If we don't give it to them purposefully, we all know they will reach in and take it, not always in the best way. They look at relationships and we see sex. They hope for love and we might see broken hearts and midnight tears. And in reality, all of those will happen for our daughters. We cannot control when, but we can influence it.

For example, study after study shows that girls who date someone their same age (within a year) are less likely to have pressured sex. In teens, boys are still developmentally about two years behind girls. So generally it's safer for girls to date boys their age or younger, and more risky, sexually, when dating someone more than two years older than them. As a parent, we have a right to put boundaries out about who she dates. So can you say, "You can date guys who are in your grade, but not older and here's why. . . ." That is completely your right and your job. Giving an explanation is important. Making it an edict without a conversation about the whys will almost ensure that she'll want to jump that fence faster than a horse in a cross-country race.

Girls who show that their sense of self is internally driven rather than externally driven are less likely to make sexual decisions based on what their date wants. By the time she wants to date, you hopefully have a good sense of your daughter and know how self-directed she tends to be. Can she stand up for herself with others (other than you)? Has she been able to navigate conflict with her girl friends or does it seem like she's always acquiescing no matter what she wants? The girl who knows how to say, "No, I'm not interested," will be better able to say that to a boy. Does your daughter have the basic sexual facts? Trust us, she needs to know that no boy has ever died or exploded from blue balls. (Note from Gretchen: When I teach my college course in sexuality, that question consistently comes up from both the men and women! At the age of nineteen, they don't know what causes blue balls, whether or not damage can be done if sex doesn't happen, and they don't know that masturbating is a sure way to relieve the testicular congestion! So don't assume that your daughter will know what a college student doesn't, unless you've told her.)

What does your daughter understand about the intersection of love and sex? Because of the female drive to connect, if she believes that having sex is the ultimate connection, then she will be more vulnerable to have sex when what she really wants is emotional intimacy. Some parents fear that if we suggest that love can occur without sex, and sex can occur without love, we give our daughters the keys to sexual debauchery. That simply isn't true. Give your daughter the ability to differentiate between what she wants (connection, intimacy, sexual excitement) and what her teen boyfriend usually wants, which brain research says is sex. Male brains have double the space and processing power devoted to sex as female brains do. Hence the conflict between females/connection and males/sex. When she clearly understands and can differentiate between intimacy, connection, and sex, she is more likely to pick the one that she wants. And that may not be sex, even when her teen partner wants it. That helps her make better decisions for herself. More than anything, we don't want our daughters to have "regret sex."

Hopefully this type of conversation started when she was a child and we taught her about her body boundaries, listening to herself rather than always going with the flow, and integrating self-respect. But now is never too late to have this conversation.

Much has changed in dating practices since we were teens. Currently teens tend to go out in groups and then split off into couples. There is less "formal" dating—where the boy picks up the girl, heads out to a movie and pizza, and then drops her off at midnight. Parents may have a false sense of safety thinking that the group will prevent the date from becoming more sexual. Further, this often means that parents may not be aware of their daughter actually having a date or having feelings for a boy at all. As dating changed, so did the language. The term *hooking up* flows like water among our teens and college-age sons and daughters. Again, when I ask my class of one hundred students to define this term, they come up with a vast list of very different behaviors. So if a guy asks your daughter if she wants to hook up, she may not know what he means. If she says yes, she may feel like she committed to more physical contact than she wants. For some, hooking up just means meeting somewhere. For others, it means kissing and petting, and others understand it as intercourse. The difference matters. If you casually ask her what it means in her school, it may start a really important conversation that neither of you will regret.

Does it seem like this age just keeps bringing more and more challenges? Well, here's another. If your daughter is dating, have you talked with her about contraceptives and disease protection? Even if she is not having intercourse, there are risks to oral sex, as far as transmission of some sexually transmitted infections. Someone has to give her the truth about her health, safe sex, and contraception. As noted in the Youth Risk Behavior Surveillance (YRBS), up to 39 percent of college students are sexual but not using protection or contraception. None of us want our daughters to be exposed to lifelong or fertility-compromising STIs or unwanted pregnancies. The conversation about contraceptives and sexual health is as central to the pre-dating period as is the discussion about seatbelts and driving. It's a difficult discussion for some of us but a critical discussion for our daughters' health and safety. If you are a dad who is willing to help your daughter get condoms for disease protection, or birth control, here's a little good news about that. Women who are on "the pill" often experience a decline in sex drive because birth control suppresses the ovaries' production of androgens, and androgens push our desire level higher. Is that a silver lining to a possibly awkward moment? Maybe. Also, women who are on oral contraceptives have a lower rate of ovarian cancer across their lifetime . . . another little-known benefit. But for your daughter, these are not the most important benefits. Her health in the moment, her ability to stay on track with her life and meet her goals and to avoid contracting viruses that could stay with her for a lifetime, or result in an unwanted pregnancy, are invaluable.

One thing we all know, as parents, is that with dating will come some level of physical touch. Holding hands, kissing, petting is the order that many of us experienced. Third base was only for the serious couples who wore each other's class ring or were officially "going steady." This is no longer the way it happens in many of our teens' lives. We are learning more about levels of sexual behavior through surveys like the YRBS. Some surveys suggest that oral sex is not at all uncommon among middle school kids, and it is almost always female to male. Dr. Roni Cohen-Sandler interviewed teen girls and found that they viewed giving oral sex as a way to hold on to their virginity, to avoid pregnancy, and to not have sex. This is a relatively new and fearsome orientation for this age group. Dr. Cohen-Sandler found that teens are often skipping first and second base and going from kissing to oral sex. With this sort of expectation or pressure, the girl who knows herself, who has a sense of her internal values, who can say "No, I don't think I want to do that" to a boy, and who can hold on to her sense of self is more likely to engage only in a level of touch that really feels right for her.

As a dad, as the first male she really has admired and trusted, you might want to prepare her for the dating scene ahead of time:

- Talk to her about her long-term goals. Getting pregnant would likely derail those goals. Your support of her goals, even as they change, will help her realize that making a less than good decision sexually now could lead to the end of those goals.
- Talk to her about the sad truth of the sexual double standard. Despite efforts to reverse it, the belief still seems to be out there that girls who give in are not girls you want in a relationship. Further, girls who are sexually available often get called a slut or easy. Boys don't get labeled like that. Girls pay the price while the boys get the high fives.
- Talk to her about sexual myths. If she says no, he will not get blue balls and explode. If she says yes, he won't love her more. If he wants sex, he is not giving her a golden ticket to a relationship or love. Those are very different things for guys. Sex is sex and love is love and sometimes they coexist, but not as much for teen boys as for mature men.
- Unlink love and sex. This may be a hard one. It may feel jaded. But if your daughter understands that sexual urges can be separated and dealt with on one's own time (i.e., masturbation), then there is an alternative way for her and her date as well, to take care of their own urges and not rely on someone else to relieve them. It may feel awfully Grinch-like to say, "Just because he wants sex doesn't mean he wants you," but it is the truth, and knowing that she might be used as a means to an end might help her be clear and better decide what she wants to do with her body and her heart.

- Be sure she has language to decline. This may mean you say, "Tell him your dad will string him up if you have sex with him." Seriously, practicing ways to say "no" will make it easier for her in the moment.
- Remind her of her own values.
- Remind her that if she thinks she has to have sex to "keep" him, he may not be worth keeping. Remind her that she is worth keeping for who she is, not what she gives.

Don't wait to set up expectations of behavior, boundaries, and rules. But first, how do you know if your daughter is ready to date? There is no single hard-and-fast answer to that. It will rest with you and her mom to decide when you let her date. Yet here are some elements to take into consideration about dating readiness:

- Some suggest that girls not date until they are fifteen years old.
- Have you talked to her about her decision making?
- Do you know, or have you talked with her to get a sense of, the strength of her internal values? If she does not have them well integrated, she is more likely to fall sway to what others want of her than she is to be able to say, "That's not what I want."
- Has she made strong friendships, nonsexual relationships with boys? If so, she is likely more comfortable being herself in their company.
- Has she respected curfews and time limits on other occasions, like when with her girlfriends, going to the movies, or to the mall?
- Has she had any previous issues with drug or alcohol use? Sadly, girls who are under the influence are simply more vulnerable to date rape and other very bad things happening in a sexual context.

It's best if you had the talk about how old she needs to be before she can date in groups and in couples long before she's ready. It's okay if you haven't. Simple rules—like your date comes to the door to get you, you are expected home on time, he does not go to your room if I'm not home, or your own versions of those—set the frame for how you will support her in this phase and what is off limits. You are allowed, as a dad, to disallow things in your home, in your car, and with your child. We talk about boundaries in greater depth in the next chapter, so read on. And Dad, never underestimate the role you have in helping her develop her own values, to set her own boundaries, and to have it from the horse's mouth that boys who care will stick around despite what physical hoops they decide to approach together.

Day-to-Day Details of Having a Teen Daughter

Shopping and Caring for Bras

She's going to need bras and lots of them because her body is changing pretty quickly. We suggest that this really is one of the times when you ask one of the women in your network (an aunt, best friend's mom, older sister) and send them off with a bit of cash or your credit card and let them do the shopping. Remind that woman that you approve of age-appropriate styles. No thirteen-year-old needs a push-up bra. Period. End of discussion. Many younger girls like slightly lined or slightly padded (and I mean *slightly* here) bras to provide them with some modesty measures. Remember why you spent so much time in the frozen-food section of the grocery as a teen? So don't freak out if you notice while doing the laundry that there is slight cup lining. It's about modesty and personal comfort.

If you have not actually purchased a bra lately, bras can cost from approximately $25.00 on up. The average cost of a bra today is somewhere between $35.00 and $55.00. Gulp. That's not for the "special" bras. That's just for a good day-to-day bra. Look for a lingerie outlet near you where really good deals can be found. Still, in most of those cases, having a seasoned bra-shopper along to comment on fit and durability is important. If your daughter engages in sports, she really will feel more comfortable wearing a good athletic bra. Like your athletic supporters, a bra designed for high activity is an important part of her uniform, competition wear, or running gear.

Bras will wear longer if they are cared for, especially during the laundering process. Here are some suggestions, as we imagine you will be doing the laundry nine out of ten times:

- Go to your local big box or bath store and buy a small lingerie laundry bag. It's a small mesh bag that you put all gentles (bras, any panties that might snag on other clothes) in before dropping in the washing machine. The bag protects bras from getting caught around the washer's rotating center and from snagging on other pieces of clothing. Before putting bras in the bag, fasten the back of the bra as it would be if someone was wearing it. The hooks will be engaged and won't snag other clothing, or other parts of the bra. Some bra makers insist that their bras should not be machine washed. We say, "Phhhaaa." If the bra is that delicate, it's not a bra for a fifteen-year-old. The lingerie bag, normal soap, and a gentle or moderate cycle will do just fine. And remember, these bras are not usually around for a long time. Your daughter is growing. She'll grow out of it before it wears out.

- In general, don't machine-dry bras. They do fine if they are taken out of the laundry bags and hung overnight to dry.
- If your daughter wants to be completely in charge of caring for her bras, fine. It might be a privacy measure. We bet she'll grow out of that and toss them in the laundry at some point.

More Menstrual Odds and Ends

Inevitably, your daughter will have several "floods" or leaking of menstrual fluids onto her clothes, and more often onto her pajamas, underwear, sheets, and comforters. This is sort of similar but not exactly equal to those sneaky visitors, the nocturnal emissions (you remember wet dreams). In the early years of menstruation, before a girl's body is fully transitioned into a regular cycle, her menses are often a surprise because they can be very irregular. So they can show up as an unexpected visitor, like the second cousins from out west. Needless to say, this is really embarrassing.

Girls new to menstruation will feel safer if they have a change of clothing stashed somewhere at school, maybe in the nurse's office. There is no glory in wandering the halls with red stains on the back of a pair of jeans. Talk to the nurse to see if this is possible. Then, if she feels like she's been set upon by her period unexpectedly, she has a private space to go rather than having to figure out how to grab her whole backpack and head to the girl's room without notice. Early on, be understanding. Accidents happen, not due to poor planning but due to wacky hormonal shifts. I don't know of a single woman or girl who has not had more than one unplanned visit resulting in some leaking.

This takes us to laundry skills. Even if she wants to do her own laundry, it would be smart of you to have a quick chat and tell her that hot water sets menstrual stains. In fact, with clothes, it's really smart to soak them briefly in cold water with some soap first or stain remover, and then run them through a cycle. Don't toss them in the dryer until you're sure the stain is gone. Once the stain is dried on in a drying process, it is set. All of the brands of stain sticks and gels available in the grocery should work as a good prewash, as long as it says that it gets out blood or protein-based stains.

When leakage occurs during the night, most of the work happens the next morning. The bed should be checked for stains including bottom and top sheet, mattress pad, pillowcases, and other bedding such as blankets or duvets. Stains that go unnoticed not only set into the fabric but can also smell of the blood component found in menstrual fluid. Getting these sheets in the laundry quickly increases the likelihood that the stains will be completely washed out.

After the laundry is started, give your daughter a hug and remind her that it's okay, that all bodies are adjusting and stuff like this happens and it's nothing to be embarrassed about. She doesn't need to hide the sheets or the jeans, and better yet, the sooner you guys get to it, the less of a problem it becomes.

Cramps!!!!!!

When a girl is menstruating, the lining of the uterus is being sloughed. Sloughed is a nice word for being biologically ripped off the wall of the uterus so it can be, through cramping, released from the body. Sounds fun, right? The uterus contracts over and over again, much like it does during labor, but less intensely. To some of us, it doesn't feel too far off from labor pains. At times, these contractions become pretty uncomfortable cramps. Some young girls, during the first few years of menses, can have some pretty formidable cramps, sending them to the couch with a heating pad and tea. The intensity of the cramps very often calms down as the body regulates, but almost every woman experiences pretty significant (read *painful*) cramping during her lifetime. Most often the most painful cramps come just hours before a period or at the start of flow for the first two days, and they then subside. Some things that help cramps are:

- Exercise. Studies show that girls who exercise regularly have lighter cramps, and that exercising when cramps come is not a bad idea. Some women find that slower exercises like yoga help. Others prefer to go for a run. It's possible that the exercise itself takes our minds off the pain, as well as releases feel-good hormones. In any event, women who exercise regularly have fewer debilitating cramps.
- Couch time. Yes, it contradicts what I just wrote, but life is full of contradictions. For some girls, cramps come with menstrual headaches, body aches, and an overall sense of lethargy. So taking a nap is sometimes just what the doctor ordered. Spending a day on the couch reading or watching old movies with a heating pad is not a bad thing.
- Laying a warm heating pad on the lower belly helps. Keep one around, as it will be a welcome option. Also hot showers or baths can relieve the pain. Some women also experience significant lower backaches. Heating pads or those little adhesive heat wraps that you can get in your pharmacy can help since they can be worn at night and during school, delivering consistent warmth to painful bellies and backs.
- Teas. There are some herbal teas available in health- and whole-food stores that say they help with cramps. Having used some, we think they might

just do that. Even if they don't, they are warm and go down nice with the range of dark chocolates often eaten in quantity during menstruation.

- Over-the-counter pain relievers help with cramps quite effectively in most cases. Those containing naproxen sodium are especially helpful, as they also lessen the heaviness of the flow without prolonging the overall menstrual event. Let your daughter try out a few of these, even the ones marketed as menstrual pain relievers. Many women have used them and found them to be helpful.

- Yes, she does feel fatter, and the truth is that in the days leading up to menstruation, a woman can gain 5–7 lbs of water weight, so that bloating she feels is real, is uncomfortable, and will leave her by the end of the period. So common sense says this is not a good time to shop for new jeans, nor is it a good time to say, "Well yeah, sweetie, you do look a little puffier." Just smile and nod, offer a cup of tea and pass the dark chocolate, and remind her that her body will feel differently in a matter of days.

- Speaking of which, some women actually crave salts while others crave sweets. If suddenly your daughter is clubbing the woman next to you in the chips aisle because she took the last bag of salt and vinegar chips, just walk her out of there and run to the mini-mart, where there is always an ample selection of bad salty foods for menstrual women.

- Menstrual headaches and their nasty big sisters, the menstrual migraines, are further responses to the fairly profound hormonal shifts that occur at the start of a menstrual period. If your daughter has headaches, over-the-counter headache relievers will help. If she seems to be developing menstrual migraines, with auras, visual changes, or vomiting, we suggest you consult with her pediatrician, who may have some suggestions for minimizing them and helping you both get through them.

- Breast tenderness is another real symptom. Young girls who are always on the move, kicking around a soccer ball, chasing a field hockey opponent, stretching out to get that backhand crosscourt drop, or running track, are often likely to feel some real discomfort. Some girls choose to wear extra-supportive bras, or they might double up on layers of camisoles and bras. The pain is real and she is sensitive. Sometimes decreasing the amount of caffeine (coffee, caffeinated sodas, and even chocolate) prior to menstruation can relieve some of this pain. Some women find that cutting back on their salt intake prior to menses helps, because it decreases water retention, which can cause bloating and discomfort. Most importantly, this will likely be a trial-and-error learning curve, as is most of the adjustment to menstruation.

All in all, this really can be a physically and emotionally taxing time for your daughter. One month she can have a great, uneventful period, and the next is a horror show of heavy cramping, heavy bleeding, flooding, and emotional swings. Remember. This is a temporary process; the symptoms should remit in three to four days in general, and she's probably no happier than you are to be going through this. Hugs, tea, and sympathy really do help. Jokes, minimization, and anger tend not to.

The Razor's Edge: Shaving, Waxing, Plucking

Around about the time a girl starts becoming aware of the changes in her body, she's likely also going to notice that some girls, or slightly older girls, have started shaving their legs. Especially if your daughter has dark hair on her legs or she has started shaving her armpits, she's likely going to start looking at the razors in the grocery store with a lingering curiosity. Some girls take the task on themselves, which can be slightly to moderately, well, dangerous if undertaken without direction the first time it's done. Think back about the first time you shaved. You had likely watched an older male shave, more than once, watched as he foamed up and carved through the froth along the curve of the neck and over the bones of the chin. For girls it can be a little different because many women shave while in the shower, so it's not such a public-access event. Your daughter may never have seen any woman shave her legs before she, herself, first drags that sharp little disposable, or better yet, your good triple-bladed razor, across her shins and knee caps. Let us just say one word. *Ouch.* There's a lot to learn about shaving legs, and though some of you dads probably know how to do it and might do it yourself if you are a cyclist or athlete, most of you haven't shaved legs.

When is the right time to start shaving legs? Well, the right time to talk about it is the first warm weather (summer?) after she gets her period. It just makes sense to have the talk before swimsuit season. This is one of those times you really do want a female figure to help your daughter out, show her the ropes, understand how to avoid slicing up that tender skin around her ankles, and razor safety 101. These days, trimming other hair growths is a pretty public conversation, as evident by the influx of bikini-line commercials in late spring. This is definitely a conversation best had woman to woman. Again there are issues of safety, consideration of why that young woman thinks she needs to trim her bikini line, or more. This is often a result of either her wearing bathing suits that are too revealing for a girl her age or her overhearing comments bantered about by older teens.

Often leg shaving really triggers parents' anxiety. It carries with it an indication of increased sexual awareness and attraction on the part of a daughter who last summer only cared about what kind of soccer socks she wore with her cleats. It can send some shivers up and down a parent's spine, because at this age, there is really no other reason to shave legs other than to look like bigger girls, sexy girls, girls who are tossing their hats in the ring of crushes, dating, and all things that scare parents. Take a breath; talk to her mom if you can. Let these two deal with this one. If she does not have a mom, access a friend/sister/pediatrician that you have assembled in your network and ask them for direction, insight, and help.

There are depilatories (lotions) that are much easier than shaving for younger girls. You can buy them in the personal care section of your grocery or pharmacy, and they work. The directions are pretty simple and they don't hurt. If your daughter has sensitive skin, she might find them irritating, but generally leg skin is that not sensitive. Pick some up and bring it to her attention. It might prevent uncomfortable nicking and cuts that often happen with those first few episodes of leg shaving.

Now a word about waxing. Waxing should only be done in a salon by trained estheticians. Wax is hot. It can burn skin, especially tender skin like brows and bikini lines. Home waxing kits ask you to first apply hot wax, and then rip it off, inflicting pain on yourself over and over again. It just doesn't seem like something that makes sense for a teen. So don't cut corners and buy her a home waxing kit. If your daughter asks you about getting her legs waxed, consider the cost (it's not cheap), but it does last longer than shaving, so it may be something to consider before a long vacation. Any other body waxing, beyond legs and eyebrows for later teens, is just not a good idea. It requires nonessential exposure of private body parts to an adult (not good for any child), it suggests increased sexuality that is likely ahead of her psychological readiness, and really, we say, "Just say no."

On Pins and Needles

These days body piercing and tattoos are everywhere. The important thing to realize is that parents should protect their teens from making permanent decisions with temporary brains. We are learning more and more about the developmental rate of teen and early adult brains. The conclusion seems to be that essentially our brains are not finished developing until our early twenties. Before then, things like impulsivity and imbalanced decision-making are the soup de' jour. Tattoos are permanent. Teen brains are temporary. Like pierced eyebrows, tongues, and those heinous big expanders inserted into earlobes to stretch them out so later a small bird can fly through the flapping gaping skin hole, they make impressions on others. Teens, however, in their drive to rebel and disconnect from "judgmental adult others," can make permanent changes that will follow them to boardrooms, business meetings, and graduate school interviews.

I once knew a young college student whose face was tattooed, his lips were pierced multiple times, and his eyebrows looked like a knitting needle factory had exploded and he was carrying shrapnel in his brows and ears. He had so much metal on his head that I wondered if he was safe during a lightning storm. Quite simply, his appearance was scary and my five-year-old wouldn't go out if he was outside. One day we had a chance to talk while taking out garbage or something and he showed himself to be a really bright, quite kind, and lovely guy. But if I had met him over an interview desk, I don't know that I could imagine him selling my product or representing my company. Ironically, he mentioned to me that he was trying to follow his dream of working in the medical field but was running up against resistance as many medical schools and hospitals had strict codes about the number and location of piercings and tattoos that employees and medical techs, physicians, and healthcare providers could, at any time, show. I can only imagine what it might be like to wake up from anesthesia in that fuzzy state and see a completely tattooed and pierced face. Like it or not, in our mainstream culture, we do judge people by these things. It's why we buy interview clothes. It's why we get our hair cut. Oddly, teens can in one moment want $100 dollar jeans to fit in while getting big obvious tattoos to stand apart. Most tattoo parlors don't allow people under eighteen to get tattoos. However, there are exceptions and alternatives. Talk to your daughter about this. Talk to her about her thoughts on getting her tongue pierced (which, by the way, is really used only as a sexual stimulator while giving oral sex). Don't hesitate to say, "Heck no, I won't pay $5,000 dollar for braces when you're about to wreck your bite and teeth with that ball you want in your tongue!" Tweens and teens, for the most part, do still want our respect and love. Speak your mind about waiting to make these permanent decisions about their bodies.

A creative alternative to permanent tattoos are traditional henna tattoos that are used in wedding rituals on Indian brides. The tops of both hands are "tattooed" with henna-colored designs, often patterns of leaves and botanical images. The good news is that they wear off after about a week or ten days. Sometimes the use of tattoo decals that often wash off fit the bill of wanting something without carving it into your skin at the age of thirteen or so.

No matter what decisions you've made about tattoos for yourself, be the advocate for sound decision-making. Remind her that she doesn't even like the sweater she just had to have two months ago, let alone the haircut she got last time and cried over for a day and a half. This is not the time to make such a permanent decision. It's okay to just say, "No way, honey!" And don't even get us started on the increase in young girls getting silicone implants . . . *arrrrrgggggghhhhhhh.*

Daddy! I Have a Huge Zit!

Oy vey, acne. It's the ruin of many otherwise fine teen days. Our skin is not only our largest organ but also our only visible organ system, so when it's on the warpath, we can't hide it as well. It's easier to hide flatulence than it is to hide a huge, red, angry zit. And to top it off, for girls, acne flares up with the hormonal rollercoaster of adolescence, and monthly with impending periods. It's a nasty little coincidence that the time of the month you feel most vulnerable and emotional and crampy is the same time that zits grow like mushrooms off a fallen pine trunk.

What's a father to do? Well, this is one of those areas where you can shine, can be aware enough to help her minimize the zitstravaganza, so to speak. There are lots of products on the market to help with acne control. The most essential steps are keeping skin clean, not over-drying with heavy acne topical cream use, and if acne is persistent and troublesome, getting medical advice from her pediatrician. There may be topical creams that she can try before you call your primary-care provider and ask for a referral to a dermatologist. In the meanwhile, there are a few home remedies that might be useful when the occasional pimple shows up.

- Warm compresses repeatedly applied to the spot the night before may help the swelling go down.
- Dabbing toothpaste on a pimple, the white kind, before bed can result in a much smaller zit in the morning.
- Eye drops that "get the red out" are a very useful tool. If a pimple is really red, take a cotton ball or Q-tip and get the end wet with the fluid. Dab it on the reddened area. Let it sit. The redness will either lessen or subside fairly shortly. Check and see if your daughter is allowed to bring this to school so she can dab it on during the day.
- If your daughter has popped the pimple, suggest she put Neosporin on it quickly. That will decrease the potential for scarring.
- Uncooked oatmeal mixed with warm water is a great do-it-yourself facial scrub for teen girls. If your daughter has dry skin, mash a ripe avocado and let her put it on her skin like a mask for five or so minutes. The

natural and gentle oils will calm the dryness, and it's just fun to mash up food.

- Plain yogurt smoothed on following the oatmeal scrub is a good and inexpensive face mask for even sensitive skin. It will help her skin clear up and stay clear.
- Acne is not connected with eating chocolate. It's primarily hormone or stress related. However, frequently eating foods like cantaloupe and watermelon are reported to help keep skin clear.

We promise you, if you take your daughter to check out an age-appropriate skincare counter or product line (many young girls like Clinique, Aveeno, Nivea, or Proactive lines of cleansers, moisturizers, and face masks), your daughter may well think you have hung the moon and the stars. You shouldn't head to the expensive end of the skincare lines for this one. Look for lines that have sunblock in their moisturizers. Look for words like *gentle*. Girls with acne often want to go in like a team of Navy Seals and bomb the heck out of their faces, picking acne till it's begging for mercy. Unfortunately, picking and then overusing drying solutions will only aggravate the problem and lead to scarring. Early skincare practices can both moderate breakouts and habituate good care for the long term.

If she tells you that her acne is getting worse or is not responding to her cleansing and care routine, ask if she'd like to talk to the pediatrician. The emotional toll acne takes on a developing teen is high. It can lead to low self-esteem, social isolation, and some nasty wisecracks from peers and siblings. The sooner she has a way to mitigate the breakouts and treat them in healthy ways when they do come, the less damage will happen to both her skin and her self-esteem.

Teasing

Louanne Brizendine, M.D., reminds us in her book *The Male Brain* that boys and men more frequently engage in verbal teasing of one another and their sisters than vice versa. In fact, even grown men are more likely to tease more frequently than are their female adult counterparts. And if you had older siblings, you might remember how harsh teasing can quickly become. When a brother is mad at a sister, all bets are off; the banter can go quickly from funny and general to laser sharp and devastating. Unfortunately for both boys and girls, the teen years offer more than enough meat for the grinder. From voice cracking to breasts budding to crushes, making or not making teams, and acne, it's a rich world for picking on one another. As a parent, understand that your teen daughter, due to her drive to connect, takes the teasing far more seriously than her brothers will. At certain times in her cycle, she is more sensitive to facial cues and tone of voice than usual so she can easily react more strongly or feel more hurt by passing digs. Some families encourage this type of painful banter. Some parents even engage in it. Teasing about body development, weight, shape, and size, as well as attractiveness or intelligence is especially painful when it comes from a parent or is ignored by a parent. This is not the time to look away or, worse, giggle and say, "That's just your brother." Maybe instead say, "Michael, as her brother and dad, we need to be in your sister's corner, not stabbing her in the back." Teasing sets a tone of background aggression in a household, which interferes with the development of trust and communication. Seems to us that if you ever wanted to strengthen your children's understanding that home is a very safe place, it would be in their teens. So be a good dad and step in when you hear the teasing start.

If after reading this chapter you are overwhelmed by the changes in teen girls, you're not alone. This is by no means the end of what you will learn about your daughter and likely about yourself as she goes through this phase. We believe that if you expect the worst out of your daughter in her teens, that's what she'll give you. If, on the other hand, you go in with an understanding that it's a time of rapid change, testing, and preparation for adulthood, then you'll all fare better. Have expectations of her and tell her what they are. Be ready to feel the pangs of sadness when she walks out the door on a date. This is the prelaunch phase. The shuttle is loaded and on the launch pads. The rockets are firing and she's about to start the countdown. How she lifts off is directly connected to how you two do the prelaunch checklist. You still have an incredibly important role in her life. Don't step back yet. Stay close. Negotiate sometimes; hold fast at others. She'll love you every moment—except when she's hating you—for your support, presence, and guidance, as well as your understanding of her cramps and need for dark chocolate. Don't be too hard on yourself, and don't forget to laugh because, goodness knows, there will be plenty to laugh at.

Adapting to Shared Custody

THE WORK of dividing a child's time between households and parents is no easy task. There are often competing interests and arguments over timing during the school year, over the summer, and on holidays. In most cases, the children, depending on their ages, are not consulted by the court system, so they find themselves and their lives being somewhat scheduled by someone who doesn't even know them. In part, this is because no judge in their right mind wants to ask a thirteen-year-old to choose which parent they want to spend winter break with. It puts the child exactly where she shouldn't be, which is torn between parents. So get ready for many elements of the custody adjustment to be bumpy. Please remember to keep the kids out of the way and try as best you can to deal with this parent to parent. Mediators are cheaper than lawyers, if you have found that you need to keep revisiting this issue.

It's possible that you and your ex were so caught up in the battle of ending your own relationship that custody was decided more by the court than by the two of you. That is the least desirable case scenario because it indicates a very high level of active conflict between two adults and an inability to come to agreement about how to co-parent the children. Perhaps, though, you two were able to come to some mutual decisions about the amount of time each of you had the children. Maybe you were even able to get a sense from the children about a schedule. In general, children tend to adjust better to custodial arrangements that help establish consistency and stability for them during the school week. Less movement between homes is preferable. Some children adjust well to splitting the week; others prefer to be in one home for a week, and then the other for a week. The most difficult thing for kids is every other night at a different house. It's simply too confusing to remember where they left their science book and it's harder for their friends to know where to find them.

Beyond the school week, weekend schedules and school-break schedules must be decided. And if two parents don't live in commuting distance to one another, some significant travel arrangements may need to be taken into account. So custody is complex on many levels. But realize that many, many children of divorce feel as if they were not asked about an essential aspect of their lives, where they are and who they spend time with. Not only do they care about time with you and their mom, but they also care about proximity to their friends, to their skating rinks, their schools, neighborhoods, the places where their lives occur.

Making Holidays, Birthdays, and Other Important Events First Doable, Then Wonderful

What we really want to stress right off the bat is that both parents need to put the child first. Especially in the first months and year after the family changed, decreasing the stress on her is an important goal. Rest assured we don't mean this to promote spoiling the child or letting her dictate the events. However, after changes of this level, children often feel supremely out of control. They don't want to go to Mom's house tonight but they have to. They don't want to spend the summer with only one parent, but the court says it's out of their control. Children who feel out of control, even teens, will find ways, sometimes challenging ways, to reassert some control over their lives. The holidays, when overall stress is high, can be over the top in stress for a teen, who has just finished her end-of-semester exams, realizes that she'll be with one parent but not both on the first night of Hanukkah, and hates her life because a huge zit has appeared on her forehead just before the Tenth Grade Snow Ball.

One way to help ease the stress is to share the custody plan that has been laid out around the holidays well before they come. Adjusting takes time. A teen who is reminded in August that this Thanksgiving will be spent in the Bahamas with Dad and not at Grandma's with Mom has time to adjust. The outline of the schedule is often a court order dictating where she is when. Parents surely will add to that by mentioning the plans to visit cousins. But building in some input from her is essential. Ask her what she'd like to do once you get to Grandma's. Would she like some time to visit that store she likes? Maybe take a few turns on the sled with her cousins? Does she want to get on the road one day or two days after the holiday is over? Is there anywhere she wants to stop along the way or does she just want to get home to spend some time with her friends? Would she like to have a sleepover a few weeks before so she and her buds can exchange gifts then? You can establish a schedule in general, which allows room for flexibility and input from the kids. Tell them in advance when you'll have them and when they are with Mom. Watch for overscheduling. If a child has to go with Mom to her local family, then friends, then Dad's family ninety miles away after returning from Mom's, that's a lot of travel, a lot of stress, and doesn't give the your teen any time to do anything she might want to do in addition to your schedule. Recognizing that the breakup of a family can double every commitment, you will see that it is the child who is doing twice the traveling. Twice the adjusting. Twice the transitions. For some children this further fosters that sense of having no control of their own lives.

If it seems like everyone else's needs are being taken care of except this poor teen who just wants to open gifts, play with a new gift, and then go skiing in the afternoon, what good is it to schlep them around? We're not saying that everything in every child's world is centered on them. They need to stay connected to family; they need to continue to feel a part of a whole. But a child with single parents can be spread too thin. Again, if the parents think ahead strategically, listen to their children, and consider their needs, then it may be that you get together for an early Christmas with the family out of state, so the kids can just balance their lives locally during a wonderful and stressful, and sometimes sad, season. Remember that by the time any big holiday comes around, we all feel stress. Imagine the stress of a child thinking about two home bases, not one. And never forget, that child has her eye on both parents, fearing that one or the other is miserable during the holidays.

There is a balanced way to ask a tween where she'd like to celebrate this Passover, Ramadan, or Christmas without putting her in the horrible situation of having to choose between Mom and Dad, or even grandparents. If you ask her thoughts on this, and then make some decisions between adults, it might go something like this:

"After listening to everyone, here's the plan Mom and I came up with: Mom and you girls have always loved the Christmas Eve thing, so you'll go to Mom's on Christmas Eve Day, be with her, go to church. I'll stop by in the afternoon to bring my famous cookies. Then early Christmas morning, after you open up gifts with Mom, I'll come get you, and we'll go skiing like we always do, then go back to our house. I'll cook dinner and we'll open our gifts then. How does that sound?"

We can't stress enough that the important part of that statement is the question, "How does that sound?" If your children respond with an alternate suggestion for how to spend your time together, listen to them. If you don't agree, listen to what they are asking for, and compromise. Our experiences are that they will often want two things: time with their friends and time with you just hanging out. Their mom may not be taking them into consideration in this way, but that's her business. Be sure not to get involved in arguing against Mom's plans for her time with the children. When you listen, and hear them, you'll come to a plan that works best.

After a few years of adjustment, trial, and error, both of us (Pat and Gretchen) are now able to share some aspect of holidays with our children and their dads. In one of our cases, we spend Christmas Eve with our daughter, watching *The Grinch Who Stole Christmas* and opening one present, our new pajamas. Early Christmas morning, Dad comes over at zero dark thirty, bearing his blueberry muffins made from Grandma's recipe. We have coffee, eat breakfast, and open gifts together. After the gifts have been opened, we eat more, lounge around, and her dad finds a place to nap. Around 11 a.m. she and her dad gather up some of her gifts and all of his and they mosey on over to his house, where they have their traditions for the day. She takes whatever gifts to whatever home she chooses, because they are hers, regardless of who gave them to her. If something like this can work for you and your ex, and it may take time for the anger or sadness of the divorce to lessen, then the benefits can outweigh any problems. It can become a new norm. It was worth the effort.

Birthdays: Yours, Your Ex's, and Hers

We hope that the court process was respectful of both you and your ex, or your lawyers were on their toes and made sure in the custody writ that your children would be with you on your birthday and with your ex on hers. If that has not been established, we are going to strongly support you both in making that a tradition. You deserve to be with your children so they can be a part of the celebration. The same goes for their mom's birthday celebration. In almost every case, children want to be able to see their parents on their birthdays. Please support your children, who will want to have some presents for their mom on her birthday and at the holidays. Hopefully she does the same for you. Even if she doesn't help your children this way, rise above and be the great father. If you are still angry at your ex and can't stomach the idea of actually shopping for her yourself with the children, give your children some cash or sit with them while they order something online and put it on your card. If they want to make something, offer to take them to the craft store, the frame shop, or the fabric store. It would be wonderful if each parent would help the kids and remind them when a parent's birthday is coming up. If you helped them before the divorce, help them after. If you reminded them before, they probably need reminders of Mother's Day and her birthday after the divorce. This is one of those times when you are showing support for your children and helping them get through this adjustment.

When a mom dies, many children will want to do something special to commemorate their mom's birthday, whether it's planting a rose bush, taking flowers and a cake to the gravesite, or going to her favorite restaurant. This is an important event for the children that reinforces that she is not forgotten and is still loved.

So what is the best way to approach celebrating the children's birthday? Ideally, you and their mom can put aside all tension and celebrate together at least enough to open gifts and have cake together. If this means putting a great deal of effort into breathing and being calm, it's a great time to do that. However, this is not always the case. The tension between adults can over-whelm the children and ruin a birthday. If that is the case, then it might be best to celebrate your daughter separately. Creating tension on her special day is harmful to her. In this case, consider making efforts to recognize her in a few different ways. Think creatively. Send her balloons to school, have flowers delivered to her, or maybe a box of chocolate-covered strawberries delivered to her at lunch in school would bring a huge and unexpected lightness to her day. Local bakeries are great with delivering cakes or cupcakes to schools, or even bake them yourself and drop them off! If she is at her mom's, call her early enough in the morning before school so you can wish her a happy day. Text her a birthday joke or song. Send her an e-card or go on YouTube, type in "silly birthday songs," and forward one to her e-mail. She wants to know you are thinking of her and there are so many ways to do it for next to noth-ing. We also suggest that what was once a birthday now becomes a birth week. The week of one's birthday is open for multiple celebrations. So if you cannot spend part of her birthday with her, very few daughters turn down another day of cake, another special meal, another round of gifts. After all, the cel-ebration of your daughter's birth can happen over and over again.

Summers and Other Holidays

The other holidays, like Memorial Day, New Year's, Fourth of July, Labor Day, school vacations, and summer break should all have been decided upon as a part of the court order. Again, it's likely that the children will have their own ideas about what they want to do, especially over summer break. Remember your summers? They were probably spent balancing activity with pure play. Maybe a week or two at camp, and the rest of the summer playing baseball on the local team, or kickball in the back lot each day. Summers have changed for our children, who often have two working parents who have prearranged the summer schedule by February of that year. Again we support conversations between the parents and the children to get a sense of what they hope for over the summer. Your daughter will want to keep her friend connections strong, and will likely want to either stay close to them, or bring them with you on your week camping, or at your home across the country. Staying in the friend loop is, simply, her priority. Spending time with you, sadly but temporarily, comes in second.

So if she leaves her hometown to be with you for the summer, help her stay connected by setting up Skype sessions for her and her friend, and not getting too worked up when she spends a lot of time texting or on the computer and the phone. Absolutely set limits, but know that she really will be much happier in your home or on your vacation with her if she can stay in contact. If possible, consider bringing her friend along on your week at the beach, or on the campout. She'll really be happier for it, and will be far more fun to be around than if she is pining for her friends. This can be a hard moment for any parent, especially if you don't see your children on a frequent basis; you may wonder why she needs a friend along to be happy. Why can't she just have fun spending time with you? Well, some girls have mentioned things like, "When I go to my dad's house, he still goes to work and I go to a tennis day camp. I'm far away from my real friends, who are all back home and having fun together." This is not about you not being good enough, fun enough, or loved enough; it's really her connection to her friends. It might warrant some important discussions between the two of you. She may well wonder why she should uproot her world when you continue yours, going to work each day. Have an honest discussion of what it means to keep a relationship going, of compromise, of sharing the time you can and how summer is one of those times.

You might ask your daughter what parts of summer she really feels she needs to be with her friends. Maybe there is an end-of-year party that happens a week after school that is a must-attend event. In some cases, the court does not give much transition time between the end of school and the day your daughter gets on the plane to your home. The court order is flexible in that you and her mom can opt to be more flexible. You can let her stay with her mom to attend the party and then fly out a day or so later. In general, if you remember that the less loss a child experiences as a result of divorce the better her adjustment, you will make some pretty solid decisions on her behalf. Granted, some of those decisions may be a little sad or painful for you. You may want to spend every minute you have with her. But if she's a teen, her job is to grow away from you a bit, to form the basis of her own adult identity; she will also spend less time with her parents in general. When this coincides with missing her through a divorce, that is painful for you. As the parent, we can be sad, we can grieve, but we still need to let normal developmental process continue.

Generally, the court simply divides up other "minor" holidays, some of which may have a lot of meaning to you. If so, work with her mom to see if you can have that day and spend time with your children on that day. This is a small but important aspect of your transition to single fatherhood. Spend Father's Day with your children. It really helps them value you as a dad, and recognize that you are worthy of celebration as well.

So consider the days that are important to you, and advocate for time with your children on those days.

Your Policy Statement

REGARDLESS OF how much time your daughter spends with you, we strongly recommend that you have expectations of family behavior that she clearly understands. Children, especially tweens and teens, tend to feel safer with a framework. No, they won't likely tell you that until they are in their late twenties, and yes, they will push back against the boundaries you set, and after all, didn't you push pack against the boundaries set for you at that age? Still, boundaries are essential to helping your daughter stay safe emotionally and physically. To put it simply, you can't know if you've gone off the property unless you know where the boundaries are.

Before we go further, we really hope that your relationship with her mom is functional and cooperative enough that you both agree on similar parenting boundaries even though you live in separate homes. Raising a daughter who knows that the rules are consistent in both houses is easier. If you don't agree with your ex about boundaries and expectations for your children, the kids can be confused or worse, they might play one parent off the other. Some kids end up favoring the parent with the looser frameworks. Often it's the dad who keeps the looser framework than the mom. It can be flattering when a daughter decides she wants to spend more time with you than her mom, but not if it's because she can twist you around her finger more easily. Your daughter loves you both, but finding the path of least resistance is not the healthy route and can, at times, allow some pretty skeptical behavior. So put that flattery away and get somewhat rock solid. Syncing both households is often easier said than done, but it is well worth the effort. You don't have to have exactly the same rules as Mom does, but it will work to everyone's advantage if there are similar rules about drinking/drug use, boys in the house, dating, curfews, earning/spending money, grade expectations, and more.

How each of you set up your household policies will be based on a lot of things like parenting styles, laws, expectations, your religious beliefs, and your ethics. So we won't begin to butt in. Let's just talk about why these boundaries are important and how to set them up as your daughter is changing, because as she grows, you may want to adjust the details and change the way they are developed.

Concrete Boundaries and Foam Boarders

As a parent, you will probably set up softer boundaries for some situations and concrete boundaries for others. Boundaries have uses. For young women specifically, one the of most salient teaching points is to learn that she can manage her own behaviors and learn that there are consequences in life. Too often females do things simply to please others. Boys follow (or break) rules and boundaries because it helps them achieve status in their group, so how you set up a boundary, and how you explain it to boys is different from how you do the same with your daughter. The boundary can be the same, but the process is not. Again, the difference lies in a girl's drive for connection. When negative behaviors threaten important connections, then girls alter their behaviors. A girl is far more likely to behave in a way to maintain your trust, to keep your respect, or, conversely, to bother you. It's all maintaining or breaking the relationship.

When setting up boundaries, be clear. What is the boundary, why, and what will it mean if she breaks the boundary. For example, a conversation might go like this:

DAD: Honey, I want you in the house by 11:00 p.m., no later.

DAUGHTER: But Dad! Nobody else has to be home by 11:00! Don't you trust me?

DAD: Yes I trust you, Annie. You've really shown me that you listen and care. Eleven is a reasonable hour for a person your age. It might not be what your other friends' parents think but it's my decision.

DAUGHTER: If you trusted me, you'd let me stay out later. I'm getting punished for behaving well!

DAD: I do trust you, Annie. I trust you because you keep to your word, you respect me, and you make good decisions. This time limit tonight does not mean I don't trust you; it's the situation I'm concerned about. That I'm letting you go the party shows that you've earned my trust. As a dad, it's my job to keep you safe, and this party, the late-night hours, the other drivers on the road, the fact that it's Memorial Day, all those factors affect my decision. Tonight's limit is 11. But maybe we can, at another time, revisit the general issue about time limits.

DAUGHTER: Thanks, Daddy. I know you love me and don't want anything to happen to me. At least I know the curfew is not because you don't trust me. But we can keep talking about it though, right?

DAD: Sure can, honey.

Now what has happened here is you have held your boundary, explained to her why you have imposed the boundary, reminded her about the impact of trust on the relationship, and given a rain check to talk at length again. And she knows you trust her but may not trust late-night drivers, partiers, or her peer group. The relationship between the two of you is intact; she gets your position (though she does not have to agree with it, she now understands that pushing this boundary now will impact your connection and your trust). You have emphasized the impact of succeeding or failing in this boundary on the effects of your relationship by explaining if she comes home on time, it will allow for some further conversations because the trust has continued to grow.

Punishments and Consequences

Most importantly, the punishment should fit the crime. These days, it seems like parents go to the default punishment for kids: taking away their phone, their iPod, and their technology. When raising girls, consider these options as some of the "big-gun" punishments, because it is their primary source of connection. Consequences are most effective if they are set relatively soon after the infraction. However, there is huge value in pausing, breathing, and thinking things through rather than immediately reacting primarily out of anger or fear. Most often, quick reactions are not good ones. The consequences are based on our emotional reaction to the infraction. Here are two examples, one of a knee-jerk parental response, one of a thoughtful response.

DAD: You were two hours late! I was scared to death! You are grounded for a week, no phone, no afternoon sports. That's it, kiddo. Things are going to change around here!

Or:

DAD: You are two hours late. You did not call me. I was scared out of my boots. I am going to take a minute and breathe, think, and calm down. When I'm ready, I'll talk to you about what your consequences are. Meanwhile, you need to go to your room and do something.

Later:

DAD: I'm ready to talk to you now about your decision to break the rules. You had a set time to be home and you did not respect that. You did not call me to let me know you would be late. I got more and more scared. Now I've calmed down a bit, given this some serious thought, and here are your consequences. No socializing for seven days. You will go to school and afternoon sports. But the minute that is over, you will come home. You will not go out this weekend during the evening. If, during this week, you are late at all, and do not call me and have a valid reason (and valid means the bus home from the soccer game has broken down), the consequences will be reconsidered and increased. Your decisions last night damaged my trust level. Any questions about the expectations?

The second option is a better one for many reasons. You have the conversation when calm. In taking that time, you let her sit and review her behaviors. That's important to her learning. The consequences connect to her behavior, not your anger or fear. A child who recognizes that also recognizes that she had options, and choosing one of the alternatives would likely have led to a different outcome. The explanation was clear, the consequences were directly linked to the behavior, and future repair (regaining trust) was laid out as a goal, and it gave clarity on how to get to that place. Remember, girls are all about connection. The rift in a connection is a significant punishment in itself. So in this example, we have the four essential aspects of effective responses:

1. Your response is directly linked to the incident. She was out late, so now she can't go out for a limited amount of time. Your response should start as soon after the incident as possible, allowing for a little time for you to think it through. Linking and response time are essential to your child's overall learning process, which is what punishment is about; it's about making an event a teachable moment.
2. You have linked the punishment to the behavior, not to her worth as a child. We all make mistakes. We all deserve a chance to repair, and that is

what parents should always give children, until they prove that they cannot manage healthy repair.

3. Your daughter understands the link between her choices (to come home late and to not call). Teaching her how to run the equation "if this, then that" is central to her making decisions for her own well-being for the long haul, rather than making decisions based on trying to please others. She learns cause and effect.

4. She understands that adhering to these consequences is, in fact, part of the repair process, in regaining your trust and regaining some level of responsibility.

Dating Boundaries

The trend these days is for younger and younger kids to "date." We want to remind you that as the adult here, you don't have to let your daughter follow this or any trend. In the olden days, when we were children, dating most often meant sitting near each other in class and maybe meeting up at the school dance, catching a smooch, and going home. Not so easy these days. With the opportunity for constant private contact on the Internet or cell phone, younger tweens and teens both are exposed to more mature relationships and can establish a "dating life" out of range of your eyes or ears. That just thickens the plot.

So back to the specifics of dating, and we're talking about the actual going out on a date. What are your thoughts, right now, when you think of your little girl going out on a date? Do you feel comfortable imagining her out, without direct parental supervision, in a public setting, perhaps a movie? Or to the beach? Will you allow her to go on a group date with six other kids to a movie? Would you let her go with a date to a school social or dance? Answering these questions will give you a read on your real internal compass as a dad. And that translates into what you will tell your daughter ahead of time. Sure there are case-by-case situations, but generally if you set up a framework, it's easier to bend the framework than it is to set one up after the horse is out of the barn. And clearly, you will shift your boundaries as she ages.

Saying No

Although saying no may be the less comfortable option, it is often a healthier option. You child may be relieved if you prevent her from going somewhere where her gut tells her she's not ready, to the basement party, or to the amusement park without parents. She may or may not tell you that, but trust us, kids appreciate being able to say, "I really want to go but my father won't let me." It helps her save face, while staying close to home. So don't be afraid to set up your expectations of dating. Figure your parental boundaries out first, then let her mom know how you're leaning, and then talk to your daughter. She'll appreciate, even if she does not agree, knowing your limits.

Co-ed Parties

Similar to dating, parties are more complex than they might appear on the surface. When would you be comfortable letting your daughter go to a co-ed party? Would you feel differently about an afternoon co-ed birthday picnic or pool party than you would a nighttime party in someone's basement? Would you feel differently if you knew that the kids would be watching the movie in the living room and a parent would always be in the room or an adjacent room? Call the parents who are hosting the party, and ask. And no, you won't be the only parent calling and asking the hosting parents, or at least I hope you're not. And if the host parents find this unusual, or seem less on top of the party than you feel is important, take that into consideration as well. They will likely be more casual and less present at the party.

What about co-ed slumber parties? They seem to be the trend among high school–aged kids, but do you think it's in your daughter's best interest to go to one at this age? Here's an editorial comment, coming to you from me, Gretchen. I really believe that we need to protect our kids when we can. And like it or not, there is a raft of societal pressure on girls to be more sexual than is age appropriate or than they are ready for. Protect the realm of the girls' slumber party as a safe space for as long as you can. When we say, "Sure you can sleep over with boys," we pull back the curtain on potential sexual behavior that she may not be ready for. I teach sexual health at the college level. I'm not afraid to talk about sex with a class full of one hundred undergrads. That aside, I have no plans to let my daughter go to a co-ed slumber party. At least until she's forty-seven years old or so. . . .

Drinking and Drug Use

Okay, it sounds simple. If your daughter is not twenty-one, then she can't legally drink. And unless you support her breaking the law, there's very little to talk about. Oh, we wish it were that simple. Clearly there are laws that clearly state the legal drinking age and drug use. Drug use, in simple language, is legal if a licensed clinician prescribes the drug to you. That's why a ten-year-old can be prescribed a morphine-based painkiller following surgery, but if you take one of those or if your nineteen-year-old mails two of them to her buddy at college, there are possible consequences. Beyond the law, you might want to look at your own use of meds, even prescription meds. If every time you have an ache or pain, your first line of defense is a pill, she'll notice that. If you borrow meds from your friends and your child sees that or overhears that, she learns. You are a role model, yet again.

You can expect that your daughter will, at some time, ask you about your drinking or drug use in your youth. If you never used substances or drank alcohol, the response is easier, but be sure not to pass up on the chance to explain why you didn't. If the reason is because you were told not to, go a little farther in your response. Include things like you didn't want to disappoint your parents, or that it was against your beliefs, or you didn't want to mess up your athletic performance. Tell her about your decision-making process. Remember, it's all about the teachable moment. After all, when your daughter is out there, on her own, she needs to have a litany of responses to lean on that work for her and that she can use in the moment.

If you did drink in your teens, be sure to remember that it's possible that the drinking age then was eighteen, so it was legal. If that was the case, tell her that. These days, with the drinking age being twenty-one, the fact that she will be breaking the law and possibly impacting things like her ability to get or keep her driver's license may be pretty important to her.

Most likely, the best way for you to respond is the way that is most honest for you, as a dad. But be sure to give her the full answer. Don't just glorify your past. Give her a context. You may want to remind her that when you were growing up, people used to smoke cigarettes, too, not knowing that it was as lethal as it is. Tell her that we knew much less about things like brain development and some of the possible longer-term effects of any particular drug than we do now. Tell her that she should make decisions that are based on what she hopes for herself, what expectations she has of herself, and who she wants to be. Tell her what you expect from her. If she will let you down by drinking, tell her that. Most teens don't resonate with broad pronouncements. The best we can do is to help her build her own healthy rock-solid foundation, and then help her put that into words. Although the expression "Just say no" was once popular, we must, as parents, help our children have a solid internal sense of good decision-making and poor decision-making. As silly as it sounds, remember that our daughters are still pushed by powerful peer norms and she wants to be a member of a group. Our goal is to help her find a pretty stable peer group, where inclusion or membership does not involve substance use and drinking.

Talk calmly with her about her decision-making process. Ask her how you can support her in making solid decisions. When she asks about your use, it's an opening to the larger conversation of how you made those decisions. The pros and cons. Your perspectives. What you thought drinking or drugs would do for you, and what the reality was. Did drinking really make you feel better about yourself? Did you struggle with your decisions? Were there negative repercussions? Did you lose friends, lose respect, lose opportunities to play sports? You don't want to make this a litany of how drugs and alcohol are bad for you, period. Add information about rates of alcoholism in your family and how that's a risk for her. Let her know how you will respond for her safety. Will you pick her up from a party if she calls and is drunk? Remind her of what you expectations are. Most children, even teens, still want to please their parents. Remember, they are connected to us, too.

Drinking, Drug Use, and Date Rape

For girls, drinking at parties and around others significantly increases the chance that someone will drop some date-rape drugs in her drink or will take sexual advantage of her while she is intoxicated. It's a sad and honest truth. A girl under the influence, whose powers of observation and self-defense are lessened, is at increased risk. She is vulnerable. Please talk to her calmly and objectively about this. The boys on the football team who treat her one way when they are sober may treat her very differently when she and they are drunk or high. Rest assured that your giving her information does not mean you are condoning drinking. This is simply real-world education and risk reduction by sharing known information. Many girls are too afraid to tell anyone that they have been assaulted because they may have been drinking or using substances at the time. Be sure to let her know that her health and safety are first and foremost in your mind. If you let her know that you will not punish her but will instead support her if she's assaulted, you'll be creating an important alliance. After she receives medical care and decides what to do legally, there will be plenty of time to discuss the situation when both of you are more comfortable. But remember, sexual assault is a traumatic event that can have long-lasting effects. You want to support her, be in her corner. At a point like that, you likely don't need to add to her burden of concerns. She will be grateful if you won't judge her, but will instead be there for her. There will be plenty of other people who judge her. Don't be one of them. You matter to her, and your response as a male role model is of major importance.

Along those lines, if she is assaulted, don't add to her fears by going after the guy. She does not need to be afraid that her coming to you has further caused problems because you want to go and beat the daylights out of the guy. She needs TLC. She need not worry that you will be arrested for assault or worse. So pull every bit of calm you can muster out of your pocket, and be there for her, calmly, lovingly, and as the best dad you can be. You can protect her in ways far more meaningful to her than by beating up someone. If she has brothers who also want to take a bat to the guy, be the dad who talks them down from that protective rush. It will not be comforting to her if anyone other than the police attends to this guy. She needs you and her family there, not in jail for assault and battery.

Finances, Allowances, and the Almighty Dollar

Teens and tweens represent a huge share of the flexible spending dollar in this country. And corporations know this, so they want to brand-up early with teens, get loyal customer bases, and get their business. There are millions of dollars that go into marketing efforts to get your daughter to spend her money on their products. Branding—or getting a teen used to using a specific brand of cosmetic/skincare, a particular line of clothing—is a huge focus. A great example of this is the development of the Pink clothing line by the Victoria's Secret Corporation. By setting up a line of pajamas, sweats, panties, and bras that are accessible and acceptable to tweens and teens, they are getting consumers like you and your daughter into their stores, which once was for adults only. It's likely that if you like their brand at fourteen, you will continue to shop their stores as an adult. When name brands are mentioned in popular songs, the music industry is involved in the branding process as well. This process can be overt, such as the development of the Pink line, or covert, like when cans of soda are shown in movies, linking the star or the character with that brand.

One very startling experience for me (Gretchen) occurred when my daughter was a Brownie. The leaders were approached by a nationally recognized tween clothing store. The manager offered to let the girls come in and choose outfits and then have an in-store fashion show. The leaders were so excited because the girls would love this idea. I put in my thoughts, feeling like the Grinch, but saying that this was not a good experience for the girls, but was rather a marketing effort targeted at creating more loyal consumers. I also mentioned that it was not going to be comfortable for girls who could not afford this more expensive store. The outing was cancelled. In this case, the well-meaning leaders had no idea how much these stores wanted to brand our daughters.

This age group is targeted because in many cases, these girls have pocket money from babysitting, helping around the house, allowances, or holiday gifts. So let's talk about how you can help your daughter learn about managing money. As she matures, you can teach her about financial decision-making and independence. Pocket money means freedom for our kids. They will need guidance, not lecturing, about how to begin to make their own decisions about money, spending, and saving.

Remember that very few middle schools teach anything about money management, so she won't know how to do it unless you model it for her. Gradual exposure to money management is a good way to start. You can help her set some saving goals, some spending parameters, and maybe at times, use your veto powers and let her know that the cost of item X is too high. Some parents do this on bigger-ticket items, like bikes, cameras, etc. We know some parents who have a 50/50 approach to spending on larger items. If a child wants a new bike but their old one is fine, the parents may say, "Okay, we'll put in 50 percent and you put in 50 percent." That teaches the child the value of earning and saving, dedicating monies and not spending immediately, and reminds them that not everything they want will be handed to them. Girls can learn a lot from gradually managing money even if it starts when they are very, very young. Establishing saving accounts early is important, and then let them gain control of a portion of that, so they can use "their money." When shopping, one test to rule out the "I want" is to ask your daughter, "Do you love it enough to spend your own money on this?" Many kids will want something desperately, until they learn they can have it if they use their own money to buy it, not yours.

Setting priorities (one pair of expensive jeans versus one pair on sale and two sweaters for the same cost of the expensive jeans) is a great teaching opportunity. For very young girls, this is also practice at simple math and boosts her self-esteem, as she is able to figure out a money-related situation.

Dads seem to struggle a bit more than moms do with a daughter's disappointment. Moms seem to be ready to build tougher girls, and dads tend to want to protect them. So take a lesson from us, and don't cave in just because she wants something. Sometimes there is valuable learning when she has to choose one rather than get two pair. It hones her decision-making skills, and she'll need them as she grows up. And if she wants something that seems frivolous, don't hesitate to say, "I know you want this, but right now you don't need it, so I'm going to let you decide if you want to spend your birthday money on this."

Allowances and Paying for Grades

We are wading into murky waters here. Parents respond differently to this issue. The singular constant, regardless of how much or whether you reward with money, is this: set very, very clear expectations on what constitutes earning the allowance. Will you give her a flat weekly or monthly rate for her discretionary spending? Or will she need to perform weekly household tasks in order to get the money? Will your child get money for cleaning their room when all that means to her is tossing stuff in the bottom of the closet? Does she get her allowance if she skips changing the cat litter two weeks in a row and you get the honor of caring for Fluffy? Remember, it's all a series of teachable moments.

If you reward her for not doing her job, what are you teaching her? Again, she will inevitably "need" something in a week when she has not "needed" to clean the cat litter or take out the trash or whatever her chore. Please do not join the ranks of people who will reward whining by caving in. It's a really bad behavior to reinforce. Her teachers, coaches, employers, and partners will thank you if you teach her that whining is not rewarded, that work and carrying her weight, holding up her end of the bargain, or planning ahead is valuable behavior.

You'll also get mixed responses from parents on the topic of paying for good grades. Some parents pay different amounts per grade. An A = $5, a B = $4, and on and on. Neither of us has rewarded our daughters with money for grades. We both believe that when a child works hard, and earns a grade in response to that work, success and self-esteem is reward enough. However, some parents do reward with money at the end of each semester. Be warned that this can become expensive, and it encourages the belief that if we work hard, someone owes us, rather than us feeling pride in our behavior. If the only motivator to do good work or deeds is "what I can get," then she is less prepared to work hard than if she knows that working hard earns her internal "goodies" that matter to her longer than the stuffed animal or the money. When motivation is internal, she will do things because she feels good about achieving things, or completing tasks, and then she'll carry that with her for the rest of her life. What happens when you're not there to pay her for her achievements? Will she have enough internal motivation to do well in her life?

Dating

BEING A single dad also means you're a single man. And at some point, you are likely to notice that you are becoming interested in dating again. You're going to get lonely, want another adult to talk to, see movies with, and share adult time. The role of father is, as we know, wonderful and exhausting. You've had a partner before and you may be looking for another. Or maybe a long-term partner is not at all what you want; all you want is, as they say, "companionship and adult company." Depending on your age and geographic location, you may have found that news of your single status spread faster than the southwestern wild fires, and everyone wants to set you up with someone. Chances are pretty good that friends have asked if they can fix you up. Maybe you've gone online and searched the Web to see who's out there, or read the personal ads in some newspapers. It's entirely possible that your children have started to say, "Dad, you need a life! What do you do when we're not here? Start dating!" Don't take that as a sign of their readiness because at that point for them, it's a concept and not a reality. Only you know when it's right for you to date. Your children may very well be at a different level of readiness and even if they seem completely on-board, or even pushy about it, that can change as things evolve.

After you've decided you're ready, the next question is "ready for what?" Do you want a long-term relationship that may end in marriage or do you just want someone to go have dinner with and a little intimacy with no real strings attached? By asking, we're not pushing you to know your future, and yes, relationships can and should have an organic "let's see how this thing develops" aspect to them. We ask because what type of relationship you're interested in will determine how you avoid the speed bumps that can come up when a parent tosses their bait back into the pond, as far as the kids go. Most children really want their parents to be happy. But many children, no matter how old, are not really interested in huge change. Your daughter may feel that there have been enough changes in her life for a while, having gone through the divorce or the death of her mom. She may be enjoying the rhythm of the house, her life. And remember, as a tween or teen, her life is a constantly changing thing from week to week depending on her social circle, her hormonal cycle, and her own interests. Sometimes kids want us to stay completely still, create no changes. They want the dock to be strong and steady and never move, so their boat moored alongside can rock with the waves and not worry about the stability of their mooring.

The balancing act is this: you cannot and should not avoid change so your daughter doesn't have to adjust. In life, the more able we are to adapt to change and remain stable, the better we'll be. You've probably never gone into the CEO's office and said, "About this merger. I'd really like it not to happen. I'm pretty set in my routine, my grasp of life at this company. And I'm thinking of buying a new home and that's really all the change I can handle, so call this thing off, will you?" The more we can help our children go through changes, intact, adjusting, and able to see the potential, the more successful they will be in life. Unfortunately, change is a painful process. And if you watched your children go through some pain during the end of your marriage, you may think they've had their fill and can take no more. Ever. But that is simply not possible. Nor is it healthy. The focus now in child development is toward emphasizing resilience. The ability to be flexible enough to manage change, bounce back, and flourish. Our children are not and should not be treated like some exotic orchid that cannot even be moved to another room. They'll certainly be better prepared for the struggles ahead if we raise them to be Timex watches ("Takes a lickin' and keeps on tickin'"), than if we treat them like Tissots that we only wear on special occasions. So if you're ready to start dating, you're ready. You have needs, too. You get to fulfill them. Just do it with some things in mind. Who you date, why you date, when you date, and how you date are centrally important to this process.

Widower or Divorced Dad—Once Again, It Matters

Remember we mentioned previously that *how you got to be a single dad impacts who you are as a single dad*? Well, that comes into play again at this point. If you are a widower, there are some different things to consider as you begin to think about meeting a new woman. The grief process is the primary issue at hand here. Do you have a sense of where you are in the grief process and where you daughter is? Generally, we mentioned that the first year is really unique and difficult. The pain is raw every day. Has at least a year passed since your wife's death? Nothing is written in stone, but boy we sure support you in using time as at least one indicator for dating in this case. We would strongly suggest that you talk to your daughter's counselor at the point you're thinking about dating again, to get her sense of where your daughter is and how to proceed. You don't need the counselor's permission but she can be a huge help in introducing the idea, guiding you at home, and helping your daughter process this change.

If you're a widower, chances are you are still living in the same home that you and the children shared with their mom. And maybe even sleeping in the same bed. Her things may still be quite present, and every nook and cranny holds a memory of her. She may have been the primary caretaker of the home atmosphere, as many mothers are. So having a new woman step into her kitchen can send chills up the spine of a child, no matter whom you bring into that kitchen, no matter when. If it's a new relationship that spurs you on to change your bedroom around or buy a new mattress, the kids are likely to feel, whether it's true or not, that this woman is pushing their mom's memory from the house. So if you are going to make some changes that the kids will notice, and boy do they notice, do it long before you ever speak about dating.

In this same vein, if you divorced and have established a new home, you have a little more leeway. The issue then can become "this is our new home and we don't want anyone else intruding." The girls may feel like they have become the mini-moms of the house. It's their domain and this clubhouse is closed to any more females. Though a comfort level that leads to a level of a sense of "this is my other home" is a good thing, children cannot rule the roost. Until we are old and no longer in control of our faculties, we remain the executive branch of the house and get last word. Teens who think they have increased power in their home are manipulative and immature and are not good household leaders. Sure they can be brought in on decisions, but parents are parents. We cannot let an angry teen set the emotional tone of the house.

We've met too many men who are literally afraid to date because they fear the negative reactions that their daughters will have if it goes far enough to integrate the woman into their lives. We've heard statements like, "I'm afraid my daughter will chew her up and spit her out!" or "I'm not going to date at all until the kids are grown and leave!" More often we hear men say, "I'm not going to introduce her to the girls until I know she's the one!" Interestingly for most women, we want to see the father in you in action before we even begin to wonder if you're the one for us. How you act around and talk about your children, especially your daughter, is a huge draw to us. So that presents a dilemma. It's possible that the woman you date may want to meet your children before you are ready to introduce them. There are lots of pieces that need to fall into place, or be gently nudged into readiness if need be. How ready are the children? How have they adjusted to the changes? How are they doing in their world (grades, sports, friendships)? Have they established a working routine, transitioning from house to house pretty well? And have you prepared them at all for the possibility that you might date someone? Take this a step at a time. Don't drop it on the children. Let them know slowly, even if they have told you it's time.

A Few Things to Consider before You Start Dating

Remember that girls are highly networked, and talk is the currency of connection. If your daughter learns that you are dating through a friend whose older sister saw you and your date at the restaurant where she waitresses, it won't go well. Your daughter will be embarrassed because she did not know that you were dating. She'll likely be in a reactive state because she's startled, and she'll feel like she's not important enough to you that you tell her in advance. In addition, if your marriage broke up because you were seeing someone else, she may tip her toes into the "Daddy's sneaking around again" pool, and you really don't want to go there. Your dating should not come as a complete sideswipe to your daughter.

We suggest this. When you know you are ready to start to date, tell her. Don't do it in a big sit down. Share the info as you're having dinner, or driving to the store for new sneakers. Maybe something like, "Hey, honey, I'm thinking I'm going to ask someone out to dinner. Nothing serious. She seems like a nice person. I'm missing adult company. At this point, I'm just starting to do the dating thing again, so it's new to me. You're important to me so I wanted you to hear it from me, not anyone else." Expect silence. Or perhaps a giggle because the thought of you dating is just a scream to your fifteen-year-old daughter. She'll chew on it for a while. She will likely come back to you with some level of comment whether it's "Who's the person?" or "What's this mean for us? Would you get married again?" or maybe "Dad, if you're dating, you're definitely going to need new clothes. Let's go shopping today! You look far too geeky in what you have! Seriously, you shouldn't go out of the house in that outfit." You might also hear, "I don't want you to date. I like our life and don't want any changes." Each of these will require a bit more response from you. Wade in slowly. Breathe frequently and often, slow, deep breaths. You may not have the answer she's looking for. When you do answer, answer the question she asked. Don't give her an answer that is bigger than the question. Here are a few suggestions.

DAUGHTER: Wait! What does this mean for our family?

DAD: All it means at this point, honey, is that when you're not with me, I may be having dinner with somebody. It's not at any point beyond that. Let's just take this slowly.

DAUGHTER: Who? Who are you asking out?

DAD: Nobody yet. I just feel ready to start dating and wanted to tell you so you wouldn't hear it through the grapevine. Steve and Bev want to set me up with her cousin. Again honey, it's just dinner. I'll keep you posted.

Or:

DAUGHTER: Great! Let's go shopping. You need a new look!

DAD: What's so wrong with the old me?!

DAUGHTER: Dad, you've been so focused on doing good for us, you need some new stuff for this new phase. You're not bad looking, but you definitely need a new haircut! Let's go!

DAD: Okay, so should I take this as an "I'm okay with this, Dad" moment?

DAUGHTER: For now. Just don't bring home anyone my age, or someone who hates kids, or my math teacher, for goodness sake. Seriously, Dad, don't date my math teacher!

DAD: I hear that. Thanks for being excited for me, honey. Let's go get you those tennis sneakers we came here for.

Or:

DAUGHTER: (Dead, cold silence. The kind that causes ice to form on the inside of windows. The kind that causes cell death. Deep freeze. You're getting freezer burn.)

DAD: Honey, you okay?

DAUGHTER: No. Not at all. I don't want to talk about this anymore.

DAD: Okay. When you're ready, I'm here. I just wanted to be the one to tell you that I'm ready to start dating.

(Dad's response here shows caring and interest, and it indicates that her silence and rejection will not shift his course. That's really important. Kids do not dictate healthy adult behavior.)

When You Date

This is a much easier issue if you share custody of your daughter with her mom because the first rule is in the beginning of dating, date when she is with her mom. Don't rearrange your daughter's schedule to accommodate your dating life. Doing that will almost guarantee that she will feel like you're shifting priorities and that she is less important to you. (Hint: If your date does not understand your role as a single dad and she puts up a fuss because you're not available to her all the time, run for the door. It won't get better.) This is not to say that you never get a sitter, but not at first, and optimally not until your daughter and this woman have met and your daughter indicates that she's okay with her.

When you talk to this person is also important. You may really like her, and want to talk to her each night. Please respect the family time and talk to her after the kids are in bed, or when they are doing their homework. Adult women will understand this. And they will likely respect you for it. Watch where you are and what you say. Little ears are everywhere and they want to see you as Dad, not flirty, sexy guy. So if you want to talk dirty, do it somewhere else or late at night when you know everyone is asleep. But believe us, you are now being watched: what you wear, how you laugh, your mood, your preoccupation when you are with them. They'll notice every text, every call, every movement you make. Keep acting like a good adult father and be prepared for some ribbing. If you get ribbing from your daughters—"Oh, Dad, you got a haircut! The dates are going well I assume?" or "Say, you never wear teal! Did she buy that sweater for you?"—that's a good sign. But make all efforts to remind the kids, at the early stages especially, that you are not changing their life with you for a woman. Even if your daughter says, "Hey, Dad, great concert in town next week. That group you really like. Why don't you ask Amy to go? We'd be okay with a sitter." Take time to explore that a little. Would all your kids be okay with a sitter? Strategically would it mean more to say, "Honey, you guys are still my priority. Maybe I can get tickets for us all and we can all go!"

or "Didn't we have family plans to see that movie that night? Good concerts come around all the time. I'll wait for the next round."

When and How to Introduce Her

This is a pretty sensitive moment, the meeting of your kids and a new woman. It's fraught with all kinds of questions and anxieties even on the best day. But there are good and not-so-good ways to do it. First off, it is better done with planning. However, let's remind ourselves that at times, the best-laid plans of mice and men are trumped by pure happenstance. Say you and your kids come around the garden aisle at the store and walk right into her. How do you navigate that? It's unplanned, you bump into one another, and she comes up and says, "Oh, Phil, are these your lovely daughters?" How will you respond, right there, with everyone watching? Well, ideally, you might have talked with your date about being a single dad and what you've told the kids and how you would want to handle an accidental introduction. The parent of the kids ideally is allowed to take the lead. Her best response would be, "Hi, Phil. Nice to see you!" because then you can decide what you might say to your kids. You could introduce them saying, "Great to see you, Amy. Where did you get that plant? Kids, this is Amy. She works in the office down the hall from mine. See ya later, Amy." Regardless, hopefully the date will let you do most of the talking. But if not, be casual. Don't overthink it; respond in a way that makes sense. You can simply say, "Yes, they sure are my wonderful daughters. We're on our way to the beach for the day. Talk to you later." Or you might say, "Hi, Amy. Kids, this is Amy. I've told you about her. Amy, my daughters, Eve and Margo." In any case, the more comfortable you are, the easier the situation will be. The kids look to you as a rudder.

Even after a brief introduction like that, you'll likely get them all together again. We suggest that you make that relatively brief, with some activity so the focus is not on the two of you or how they get along with her. If friends have introduced you, and they later throw a barbeque with lots of adults and kids, that would be a great setting, but let the kids know she'll be there, too. The kids have a distraction, they don't have to sit and focus on you, and you can interact with any number of adults. Be sure not to be all kissy-face and pressy-body in front of the kids. It will give them a chance to watch how she interacts with you from a distance, while they play kickball with their friends. If they say, "Dad, we want to leave now," listen. It means they are likely on overload and need some time with you.

Even if they really like her, this is still an adjustment. They are sharing you with her, they are recognizing that there may now be divided attention, and they are wondering if you are trying to replace their mom. Be ready to talk about these things. If your daughter is old enough to be interested in dating, remind her that this is the rhythm of life. She needs to grow and change, add people to her life, but you know you're not being replaced. Maybe she can look at it the same way. She might be relieved that you aren't alone and lonely when you don't have the kids. She might really hate this woman. The dance of adding new people to your life, and theirs, is a process. There will be issues, missteps, and emotions. That's just the stuff of life.

One more word about introducing your family to the woman you date. Please be clear about your motive. We have known men who have introduced their children to their date to impress their date. The kids reflect him and he walks them out as testament of what a good dad he is. Well, don't. If you want a chick magnet, get a puppy. If you want to do this well, take time and really think about it. Even if your new woman really wants to meet your children, it has to be at the rate the children are ready for, not because the new woman wants to be integrated into the family *now*. Adults can and should regulate themselves so they can manage waiting, anxiety, and curiosity. If you want your kids to feel like a zoo exhibit, introduce them when it's on the new woman's terms or when it works for you. If you want the children to have the most balanced sense of this, wait till you have had a chance to talk to them, you have gone out for some time, they have expressed curiosity, and you have discussed the relationship at their level. Give them a reason why you want to introduce them. It's okay to say, "I want to have her know who I'm talking about when I talk about stuff you and I do," or, "I don't want these two aspects of our lives to be so segregated." Don't be at all surprised if she says, "That's your life, Dad. I'm not dating her. She has nothing to do with me." To which you might respond, "You have everything to do with me. You're my child. I love you more than life. So if you are both in my life, there needs to be some level of a bridge. You're right, I'm dating her. But you're both in my life." If your daughter is dating she might understand this at a different level.

A few more thoughts about potholes at this point:

- Be deliberate. Don't introduce her to every woman you date.
- When you talk about her, talk about appropriate things like where she works, hobbies, things in common.
- Model boundaries. If your daughter asks if you're sleeping together, respond with, "That's not for you and I to discuss, honey."
- Don't force integration of her kids and your kids too soon.

- Watch your mood. If you and your friend are fighting, try to keep it out of the house. If you're feeling silly and giddy and in love, remember to keep being the dad, too.
- Don't talk up this woman too much. Your daughters will feel like you're selling her to them.

Who You Date

Chances are you are going to date a woman who is in proximity to you, either through work, friends, or hobbies. If you are Internet-dating the scope may expand, but even then we look for people who live near us. That means there is always the chance that there is a connection between your family and her. Maybe you find out that your kids went to the same soccer camp, or she was married to a former dental patient of yours. The commonalities sometimes make it easier to establish a relationship. However, from a kid's point of view, they can muddy the waters. It's not impossible for you to date one of their friend's moms or teachers or former coaches or old pediatrician. In general, kids have a bit of a different adjustment response when a dad starts to date someone from their world. They often think that they are all you'll talk about, or that you are now encroaching on their lives. If this arises and you meet someone with a mutual connection to you and your children, it may also mean there is a connection to your ex-wife, their mom. That certainly adds additional spice because as you're dating, they might be hearing their mom's take on the development, and not all moms will be supportive and kind to you as you move on. So you see, it can be sticky. But we're not saying it shouldn't happen or that it will never work. It does add a layer of caution. And when you are ready, after you've had enough dates to know this person is worthy of being introduced to your kids, sit down and have a really good talk first. Explain whom you're seeing, how you met, and what you and she have in common. Share a bit about stuff you've enjoyed together, like tennis or movies, so she appears more as your date than their coach. Let her know that you will not embarrass her by kissing it up on the sidelines at this weekend's state tournament, that you'd never do that. And listen to her feedback. She'll have some. This is not an impossible situation, and in many smaller towns, it can be an unavoidable situation.

Most daughters will be relieved to learn that you are dating an age-appropriate woman, not a twenty-five-year-old grad student who she can share clothes with. They don't want to hear about you and your escapades being the talk of the town. They don't want to be embarrassed when she and your date show up at the picnic wearing the same Abercrombie shorts. They don't want a scene. Teens hate scenes, they hate to be embarrassed, and they don't want to stand out in negative ways. So when you're choosing dates, remember this. Yes, she will certainly pick boys (or girls) who you may not like, who shock you, who embarrass you, but she is at a different point on the human learning curve. Also remember, if your date is highly sexualized in her appearance, it pushes issues right in your daughter's face that she would otherwise like to avoid, that you are a sexual being and are hot for this woman. A grown-up who flaunts her sexuality out and about like that, in ways that are not appropriate to age and setting, is disquieting to many, many people. Don't create a situation where your daughter questions your judgment at that level.

Sleepovers: Yours, Not Your Daughter's

So you think it's time for your date to spend the night. You've introduced her to the kids and they seem to get along. You've gone on a few outings to the water park, to a baseball game, and all's well. You and she have been dating for six months or more (an arbitrary length of time, but we'll take it) and you wonder when the kids might be okay with her sleeping over. First, this might not ever be something you would do, if your morals and ethics preclude it. Always lead with your ethics. If this is something you want to consider, here are a few suggestions:

- Tell your kids about it. Tell them a bit about your decision like, "Since we're spending more time together and you all seem to like her, I would like her to spend Saturday night here. It gives us time to hang out with you all, put you to bed, watch a movie, and not rush the night."
- You should have some clear information that your daughter likes this woman. If she doesn't, don't take this step yet. Children should not feel uncomfortable in their own home.
- You should be clear that this is a relationship that is more than just dating.
- Have her sleep in another room, and make it clear that she is, indeed, sleeping there. Don't put her in another room or say she'll be on the couch and then have the bed not look slept in. If you decide to be intimate, and we suggest you not for quite some time, lock the doors. On the first few sleepovers, the kids will watch for who sleeps where, what time you came upstairs, and how long the showers ran. The goal of the first few sleepovers is not monkey sex in the playroom.

- Don't flaunt her sleeping over. Don't let the kids find you reading the *New York Times* in bed together Sunday morning, or letting the kids wake up to her making pancakes in your shirt the next morning.
- The first sleepovers should end fairly early in the morning. She should leave soon after breakfast. It gives the family time to decompress and talk about it if needed. Your children need space as this relationship grows. They need time to digest the changes.
- Act like adults. Don't fall all over each other.
- Maintain your family rituals. If you always make pancakes, wake up the next morning and you make the pancakes. Rituals are important at this point. They suggest that even in change you remain constant.
- If this was the home that their mom lived in, please proceed slowly. It's a different process to see a new woman in Mom's kitchen, sitting in her favorite chair, or on the back porch watching the sunset.

Summary Thoughts

Maintaining your privacy through all this may be a challenge. As we've said, you're being watched like the air space over the White House. If you have dating-aged daughters, they may find great delight in playing back comments and questions that you, the parent, have posed to them, like, "Dad, we hope you're taking precautions sexually."

They may want to know where you went, what you did, if you love her, how much money she makes, and why she got divorced. The important thing for you to remember here is: you are the adult. So even if you have asked her the same questions, you did it as a parent. You didn't do it for general knowledge; you did it out of care and responsibility. As the parent, you can and should continue to model boundaries.

Sex, income, reasons for divorcing someone, dating history, drug use, and more are topics you can and should draw boundaries around in your life. Feel free to joke with her and say, "Your old man can take care of himself, thank you," or, "Geez you're a busy body about Cheryl. Slow day at school?" But don't change roles. She may be wondering if your behaviors are congruent with what you established for her. If you can have someone sleep over, why can't she? Well, you remain the adult. You remain the chief arbiter of your decision making. You have years of thoughtful deliberation, and you are considered adult in all realms. That's why you can decide differently. You are not peers. You may be engaged in the same behaviors, dating, but you are still the adult, her father, and in that there is a difference. You are meant to protect and teach her. Sure, you can learn from her every day, but you remain the adult on duty. Don't compromise that, because, really, she needs you in that role.

Remarrying, Stepkids, and the Whole Shebang

To be clear, this is a very big and very important issue. Making the decision to remarry is huge. Making it well is central to the chances that the marriage will succeed. The divorce rates for second marriages and then sequentially third, fourth, and so on, increase with each marriage. At the same time, men seem to remarry relatively quickly after a divorce or death of a spouse, much sooner than do women. We are, by no means, well versed in the issues of stepfamilies and remarriage, so we'll leave it to the experts. Needless to say the more you know, the better prepared you and your children and she and her children are, the greater the likelihood of success. We have put resources on remarriage and blended families in the bibliography at the back of this book.

However, we should mention a few things here. When you are thinking about remarrying, really ask yourself, Why now, why this woman, and who are you doing it for? If your ex is still alive, your children probably don't want, nor do they need, another mother. They might welcome a stepmom who knows that she is not replacing Mom in any way, but who adds to the village that loves your daughters. Be clear with your sweetheart. Ask her what she hopes for in her relationship with your kids. And if she has children of her own, she should be talking to you about the same things. If the adults want something for the kids that the kids don't want, you've got yourself the makings of an old-fashioned barnburner.

Don't overlook the concerns your children might have with you becoming someone else's stepdad. There could be some fears that you will like them better, that you will be a better dad to them. The kids may wonder how the day to day of their lives could be altered, like where you all live, if they have to change schools or share bedrooms, if there is still enough money for you to buy them new bikes if there are more kids in the house.

If your ex has remarried before you have—which is not likely, as men usually remarry sooner—your daughter may have already had experiences in balancing a dad and a stepdad. So for some teens, the addition of a stepmom may be old hat. For those teens whose mom has not remarried, this is a concern. Can they love their mom and still really like their stepmom? Do they have to choose families, and will anyone expect them to side with them in alliances? Be sensitive to this. It once again touches on the issues of connection. Your daughter wants to be connected. She generally does not want to reject or prioritize family members. She does not want to be asked to choose. You can have a big impact on her comfort level with the changes that are inevitable when you or her mom remarry.

Whenever families blend and there are kids from both families added into the mix, inevitably there will be times when the rub centers on issues of family loyalty: loyalty to silly things like baseball teams, loyalty to celebrations and rituals, schools, and grandparents. Speaking of grandparents, they, too, are a part of the blending, as are aunts and uncles, and they can help make it easier just as they can complicate the issues. We've heard of blended families where step-grandchildren are not acknowledged for holidays and birthdays, while the grandkids are showered with gifts and love. One set of grandparents literally didn't even acknowledge the step-grandkids at all. Not a mention, not a hug. It made the blending incredibly difficult. Access resources who can help you consider if you are ready to do this. You cannot be too prepared, too thoughtful, or too deliberate in this process. Read the books. Talk to family therapists. Maybe even go to family therapy ahead of time to prevent some problems. This is not an impossible task. But the data says that not many of us do it well enough to do it successfully. Talk to people in your community, at church or temple; talk to your friends who have done it. You don't have to blaze your own path on this one. Ask for help. It makes you a better dad, a more prepared future husband and stepparent.

This is a new step in your life. You will do it best when you're ready, when you're clear about what you are looking for (a date? a wife?). Your daughters will be watching you like a hawk and you can expect some initial negative response to your interest in women. You don't need your daughter's permission, but having her onboard on some level eases things. Think of it this way. When she dates if she said to you, "I don't care what you think!" you're going to react in a certain way, and it sure won't make life easier for either of you. So let the children know they do matter, you do still love them, you will always be Dad, and you're not trying to replace Mom. Move slowly and deliberately. The book *Dating for Dads* by Ellie Fisher, listed in the bibliography, is a valuable resource. There will be bumps, some false starts and challenges. But that's life. You can and, when you're ready, should do this. You do need a life of your own.

CHAPTER

9

Concerns, Crises,
and Interventions

WE ALL have coping mechanisms that we've picked up to manage painful emotions and events. Some of them are healthy coping mechanisms, and some, well, not so much. Generally, good coping mechanisms are balanced. We do them in moderation, with good outcome, and they have no negative side effects. Running after a hard day of work is a good way to let off steam. It releases endorphins and reduces stress. Drinking a gallon of vodka will also change our moods, but not for the better. The side effects are too many and too negative for this to be considered a healthy coping mechanism. Our kids are still amassing their toolkit of healthy coping mechanisms. The crises for teen's lives generally occur when they use ineffective coping mechanisms. Let's talk about some of the behaviors as seen in teens, especially.

Self-Harming Behaviors (Cutting, Burning)

Sadly, teen girls are not strangers to hurting themselves. If you're not familiar with self-injury, learning about it is important, but it may not be easy. If you have never injured yourself, it seems absolutely unthinkable that anyone would use a razorblade to cut their arms, their thighs, or their chests. Putting a cigarette to your wrist or carving skin with a sharp knife or razorblade is nothing short of mind-blowing to someone who has not done it. But if you have a daughter, you should know more about this disturbing behavior because it's on the rise among teens, and it is often a behavior that one girl introduces to another. The Youth Risk Behavior Surveillance (YRBS), a nationwide survey of high school students conducted through the Center for Disease Control, in 2009 noted that self-harm behaviors are ten times more likely to happen in students who have suicidal ideation. Self-harming behaviors may be different than direct suicide attempts, but cutting your body with a knife or razor can certainly be preparation for slitting your wrists vertically in hopes of dying. So if you notice new scars or old ones on your daughter's body, speak up.

You're wondering why anyone would do this, right? Well, there seem to be differing motivating reasons. Most importantly, it's a negative coping mechanism. Girls who cut themselves often cite the feeling of control and relief they get when they cut. They are in charge of their pain, when and where it happens, and this is a relief for them if they feel a larger internal sense of pain that they can't control. It's a diversion. It's like cutting into a snakebite to release venom; it hurts but less than letting the venom eat through the muscle. For each girl who cuts, the underlying question "relief from what?" will have a different answer.

While some girls cut themselves to distract themselves from other internal pain, others feel powerful and identify with their abusers when inflicting pain on themselves. Maybe it's an attention-getting behavior; in these cases the cuts or burns are on parts of their bodies that are public like forearms or lower legs. If a girl is cutting on hidden areas, and some deeply disturbed girls cut on their breasts and labial areas or upper thighs, then it's less likely to be attention getting, because it won't be as easily seen. This is an indicator of deeply disturbing emotional issues, which need rapid attention.

Self-harm behaviors are distinct from suicide attempts. Many people who are suicidal will learn about the method they are considering and know where and how and under what conditions one will die fastest from cutting their wrists or throat. Self-harming cuts tend to be reasonably superficial, though scaring can be quite obvious. They can appear on the wrist but most often not deep enough to cause someone to bleed out. Often they are horizontal rather than the more effective vertical cuts of someone who is intent on suicide.

If you notice scars or burns on her friend, talk to both her and your daughter about it. You may be the adult who notices and is willing to call it as you see it and get her help. Cutting and burning are also behaviors that girls teach one another. If her friend is doing it, your daughter may be doing it, too. If you notice these behaviors or scars on your own daughter, including persistent and deep body picking, recognize the importance of getting your daughter professional help. Start with your pediatrician. They'll know who to refer you to. Overcome your shock, your deep desire to look away or think you saw something else, talk to your daughter, and call a professional.

Eating Disorders

There are several types of eating disorders that are affecting our daughters today, and they range in severity from mild restricting and/or purging to severe anorexia or bulimia. This is a difficult time to be a young female. On one hand we are constantly barraged with the data on the rise of childhood obesity. On the other, we see photos of ultra-thin models and read stories about women who have gone to surgical extremes to alter their body shape. It's a hard time to find the balance for an adult, much less a young woman. Here are some very real and alarming data points that clearly paint a picture of why young women today are at risk to develop eating disorders:

- Over one-half of teenage girls and nearly one-third of teenage boys use unhealthy weight-control behaviors such as skipping meals, fasting, smoking cigarettes, vomiting, and taking laxatives ("Eating Disorders Statistics").
- About half of American children between first and third grades say they want to be thinner ("The Average American Woman—Dieting and Weight Statistics").
- One in four college-aged women have tried to induce vomiting, used laxatives, or are bulimic in order to manage their weight.
- Tweenzines (magazines devoted almost exclusively to standards of weight and appearance) focus on and reinforce the message that there is an acceptable weight and body type for teens. Teens develop at such differing rates, and this suggests that the proposed "norm" is off base and can set a false normal. Most fashion models in magazines are thinner than 98 percent of American women.
- The average adult female weighs 144 lbs and wears a size 12–14, yet public sources like magazines endorse women of this size as "plus-size models." The media labels normal as "fat." What is normal in real life becomes abnormal in the media. Trust us, the media has a huge effect on your daughter's sense of self.
- During the course of puberty, the average American girl will gain between 40 and 60 lbs. This weight gain is absolutely normal and necessary for the next stage of development. Girls grow out first, so then

they can grow up. The extra body fat redistributes and allows for menstruation to start. For a society clearly focused on the number on a scale, this weight gain feels awful to the girl, especially if she is developing ahead of her peer group and negative comments are made about her body. Parents, sisters, and brothers can also make mean and inappropriate body-based comments. The appearance of pudginess is an indicator of future growth, not a suggestion of obesity. In order for a girl to proceed healthily through adolescence, she needs that body fat, as fat produces estrogen. Girls without sufficient percentages of body fat will not start their menses. Just as they become aware of their appearance, our daughters will likely feel pudgy. Explain this as absolutely healthy and normal body phasing and as a transitional phase for her body. It's temporary.

- If a girl has started her menses, weight loss and restriction have the potential to halt those periods. Elite female athletes often have so little body fat that they do not have their periods. In the long run, this can affect things like fertility and vulnerability to osteoporosis. (See www .lpch.org/DiseaseHealthInfo/HealthLibrary/adolescent.)

We will review the more apparent eating disorders, bulimia and anorexia. They can occur independently of one another, but very often, anorexics have experimented with either vomiting or laxative abuse in attempt to lose weight rapidly. A hybrid disorder involves the behaviors of binging and purging as well as severe restricting. Both bulimia and anorexia are reported across almost all ethnic groups and are starting to be noted among boys and adult women as well. These disorders can be taught to girls, and there are even "pro-bulimia and anorexia disorders" websites that can walk a person through the steps of starting an eating disorder, as sad as that sounds.

Bulimia and Its Symptoms

You're pretty sure you're losing your mind. Two days ago you stocked up on groceries. Veggies, fruit, cheese and deli meats, chicken, hamburger, and some tiger shrimp for the barbeque, plenty of food to get you and the kids through the week. Tonight you notice that new jar of applesauce is missing. So you sub in corn—not as good but it will do.

Abbi, your sixteen-year-old, asks for more mashed potatoes, and she eats plenty of dinner rolls and butter, more carbs than meat. As usual, the kids split from the table as fast as humanly possible after they put down their forks. "Where's the fire? What about family time?" you call out. Abbi is at the top of the stairs before you even finished the sentence. Twenty minutes later she comes down, a little flushed, one of her eyes a little bloodshot. "You okay, sweetie? What's up with the eye?" "Oh that. I got between Sarah and the ball in field hockey today." Strange. You didn't notice that before dinner.

Abbi loves school. She is a star on her field hockey team and has a competitive streak. She talks to you about a drive to win, the drive to be the highest scorer. She's popular, always goes to the school socials, and seems to be interested in a boy on the lacrosse team. She runs daily, even after she's run with the team. She's going in early to work out. It seems to be paying off. She's kicking butt in games. You're a pretty proud field hockey dad.

Now you're done with the dishes and the counters are wiped, and the kids are doing their homework. As usual, you head to the freezer for your pregame bowls of ice cream. But where's the ice cream? You just bought it! Your favorite flavor! It's nowhere to be found. You must be kidding. First the applesauce, then the ice cream, and the sandwich bread is almost gone, too. The yogurts are gone. You opt for a little chips and salsa and a beer. Seems like nobody has busted into the chips yet.

Like most girls her age, Abbi takes her phone calls in her room and has been a bit moodier lately, but what sixteen-year-old isn't? She studies constantly and melts down when she doesn't get an A. She is focused, driven, certainly is a leader. You like that in her. She doesn't seem to be as interested in fashion because you notice her wearing baggy sweats, which seems to make sense. She is harsh on herself, always striving for perfection. She thinks she's fat, but what girl doesn't?

Soon she's back downstairs and heading out for a run. Wait, didn't she run after school? Can she be running again? When you ask her about it, she reminds you she's got a game tomorrow. She returns from her run, another four miles on top of the three she ran this morning. She's always been a pretty driven kid but this seems like a lot. She's so focused and intense, you don't know whether to be proud or worried.

Three weeks later, following a dental check-up, you get a call from Abbi's dentist. She tells you that she's noticed a pattern of dental wear that is consistent with bulimia—that's where people make themselves vomit, often several times a day, to try to minimize caloric intake and keep their weight within a certain perceived acceptable range. "You're crazy," you tell her. "Abbi is a star. She works out so much that she doesn't have to restrict her eating." "That's part of the disorder," the dentist tells you. She reminds you that this pattern of wear is only caused by the repeated exposure of stomach acids on the backsides of teeth, from repeated vomiting. How could Abbi be doing this? Why is Abbi doing this? She seems so great, so happy, and so successful.

Abbi is not alone, and in general, you have not missed anything. Bulimia is a sneaky disorder and common among girls. In general, girls with bulimia do not appear too skinny. Bulimics engage in binge or binge/purge cycles and can abuse laxatives. The goal is to keep food moving so quickly through the system that the full calorie load is not absorbed. She aims to eat all she wants, as often as she wants, without the usual weight gain. Girls might purge for weight loss or to manage emotional distress. Binges often consist of eating huge amounts of calories (some binges can be over twenty thousand calories) found in soft foods that are painless and easy to vomit like cakes, brownies, ice cream, white bread, pasta, applesauce, yogurt, puddings, Twinkies. That's why Abbi had not eaten the rough-edged chips. They would be more difficult to vomit than mashed potatoes.

Frequent vomiting has long-term negative effects on both tooth enamel and internal organs, can lead to tears in her esophagus, metabolic problems, and nutritional imbalances. Laxative abuse can also cause significant metabolic problems and may even disrupt a body's natural elimination process. If this happens, the laxative abuser's body will need to relearn to take control of its own defecation through retraining. Here are some things to look for if you are wondering if your daughter might be binging, purging, or abusing laxatives:

- Fingernails are cut short so when she sticks her finger down her throat to initiate the gag reflex, she won't scratch the back of her throat or the inside of her mouth.
- Fingers are often red and chapped-looking from the tip of the finger to the middle knuckle. This is the part of the finger shoved down the throat and often gets exposure to the stomach acids involved in vomiting. This most often occurs on the same hand that she writes with.
- Soon after eating meals she excuses herself from the table and heads to the bathroom, often the one farthest from the rest of the family.
- You might not see weight loss. At the early stages, it's more important that she experiences the ability to control her world, her stomach status. The vomiting is satisfying.
- You find soft foods stashed in her room. Binges rarely involve crackers, hard cookies, raw veggies, or things that will hurt when being vomited soon after eating. She might eat soft cakes, mashed potatoes, processed breads, ice cream. Bulimic binges can be extremely high in calories, but she doesn't mind this, as she will be throwing up in minutes. Most, if not all, of her binging occurs in private.
- You find laxatives, diet pills, or diuretics (water pills) in her room, pocketbook, schoolbag, or in the garbage.

- You notice that the softer foods are gone faster than the nonsoft foods. The ice cream, Twinkies, cupcakes, puddings, etc., are flying from the cabinets.
- Bulimia is a learned behavior. Girls often teach one another how to induce vomiting, or they go online to pro–eating disorder sites (yes, they do exist) to learn how to make themselves sick. Check her computer search history. If she has friends who are binging, purging, and abusing laxatives, she may well be experimenting.
- Some sports are well known for athletes having eating disorders because of a strict sense of body shape and thinness and weight limits. At risk are girls who participate in sports that place a high level of value on aesthetic appearance such as ballet, figure skating, and cheerleading. In cheerleading, the "flyers," or the girls who are tossed in the air, need to be tiny, and often they are encouraged to be very weight conscious. If your daughter is involved in any sport where weigh-ins are necessary or a strict body type is expected or trained for rather than strength and ability, be aware.
- Bulimics can become so effective at purging that they do not need to stick their fingers in their throats to induce vomiting, so you may not see signs of chapping on their fingers. That usually means she has been purging long enough to know how to vomit without a finger trigger.

Anorexia

Anorexia nervosa is one scary disorder. It can accompany bulimia or appear on its own. Importantly, you will have a bit of time to notice the symptoms and to intervene. Anorexia had been diagnosed exclusively among young white females in their teens and twenties until fairly recently. It is now being noted among girls in other cultures and in men. Clinicians and physicians are seeing an increase in later-onset anorexia among women in their forties and older, as well as among other ethnic groups including Latinas and African American teens. The more women are exposed to social expectations that they fit into a size 00 (that's double zero!) clothes, the more we believe that weight suggests worth, the more we focus on external rather than internal attributes, the more eating disorders flourish.

This disorder affects girls and women on many levels. It generally begins with food-restricting behaviors caused by a need to control. Often girls who develop anorexia report on a sense of feeling that their lives are completely out of control. She feels that she is never good enough, and seeks perfection. By starting to pick and choose her food selection and amount, and then seeing the impact on her body size, that girl gets a fairly immediate sense of control. Anorexia can start as a diet gone wrong and then follow its own dangerous course. Experimenting with binging and purging, bulimia, can blossom into anorexia.

Anorexia compromises every aspect of a person's health, cardiac function, menses, bone health status, mental health, her body's ability to maintain core temperature, skin and hair growth, and more. If untreated, and even following treatment, anorexia can be fatal. The longer it has a hold, the deeper the consequences and the more significant the treatment efforts.

It is the most damaging eating disorder and can persist for years. Psychologically it hinges on the young girl feeling out of control with her world, striving for perfection and then finding that controlling food is rewarding. The rewards come from friends and adults commenting on how good she looks after weight loss.

Along with changes in eating patterns and the food she eats, a young woman developing anorexia will likely increase her exercise routine, increasing aerobic exercise. Her goal is to lose weight, not to add muscle mass. She suddenly is aware of the calorie count of one brand of yogurt over another, one cereal over another, and one apple size over another. Food is no longer about pleasure or taste; it is a reflection of a drive to control something, anything, in this case, her body.

The preoccupation with food becomes intense. She may start to collect cooking or food-related objects such as cookbooks, and she might become focused on cooking for the family. However, she will often not eat the meals she cooks. She begins to pressure you to eat certain things, even when you are not hungry.

As she loses weight, she loses fat, so she becomes more sensitive to the cold. She begins layering clothing for warmth, making up for lost fat and to distract others from seeing her significant weight loss. She wants to hide her body because she only sees it as fat and ugly. She is not necessarily trying to attract attention to herself, but rather is trying to shrink, to make her world more controllable and her body smaller and smaller. If she loses enough weight, she will stop getting her period and will develop a fine downy hair covering all over her body. This is called *lanugo*, and it grows as a body is trying to compensate for lost fat to keep her warm. Her hair loses its shine and breaks easily. At this point, cardiac health can be significantly compromised. Hunger pains stop. Her moods change; she's increasingly irritable, has trouble concentrating and focusing, and may sleep more. Quite simply, she does not have enough energy for her body to function at full capacity.

Anorexia should be treated as early as possible. An experienced treatment team of a dietician, health care clinician, and therapist will likely be needed.

This is not overkill. This disorder is a hydra that needs to be approached on every level. If cardiac symptoms are evident, hospitalization is often required.

In most cases, the family is also treated. The disorder affects everyone in the family, by its controlling nature, and parents need support in helping make healthy changes as well as learning the full extent of their daughter's illness. Please understand that your involvement in her recovery is essential.

Signs and symptoms of anorexia include:

- Significantly decreased food intake.
- A preoccupation with body image, food, calories, or weight.
- Not eating in common areas, with the family, or anywhere but in private spaces. In the early phases, she may do a lot of moving her food around on her plate, so she looks like she's engaged with her food and eating, but she's not.
- Increased rituals and restriction around food prep or eating. "I have to use the same plate. I only eat with this one fork."
- Decreased variety in the foods she eats. She focuses on low- or no-calorie foods such as cucumbers, mushrooms, fat-free yogurt. Amount of intake gets more and more restricted as the disorder progresses. She is obsessed with calorie counting. One woman with anorexia we knew actually counted out the curds of low-fat cottage cheese she would put on her plate. She would eat a slice of cucumber, two slices of radish, six low-fat cottage cheese curds, and a mushroom at each meal.
- Preoccupation with exercise. Exercise is usually done in heavy sweat-shirts or clothes that will encourage sweating, including wool hats. To an anorexic, weight loss is weight loss, whether it's water weight or not. You may see her constantly moving. While she stands, she shifts from foot to foot. She does squats in the kitchen. She works her arms when sitting. Her feet are moving; she's opening and closing her hands. Any possible calorie expenditure is her goal, so she wants to continuously burn calories.
- Use of laxatives, water pills, or diet pills. If a physician or healthcare provider does not recommend these, she should not be using them. If she has them in her room, she is very possibly hiding their use.
- A change or cessation of her menses. She will stop having her period because she does not have enough body fat to generate enough estrogen for menstruation to occur. Along with weight, a medical team will assess for BMI when doing an exam as another measure of health.
- She frequently talks about her fears of gaining weight, or she talks about how fat she believes she is. At this point, it's not just talk; she's not looking for you to say, "Honey, you have no fat." She is expressing what she

sees in every single mirror. Her perceptions are so skewed that she can look like she's starving, which she is, and she sees fat.

- Development of a layer of downy fuzz on her face and body including her arms, face, legs, belly. This is an attempt to maintain core body temperature. This looks fuzzier than her normal arm hair. It has been described as looking like baby duck down.
- Wearing layers, hats, gloves, while exercising to promote more calorie loss even in warm weather. Exercise increases, despite the weather. Along with calorie counting and restricted eating, exercise is a prime focus.
- Avoiding wearing revealing clothes, bathing suits, etc.
- Lack of energy, focus, and concentration. She is literally so calorie deprived that her brain is not functioning well enough to focus and concentrate, and her body is too weak to move much. This is a suggestion of significant anorexia, because most women with anorexia will exercise as much as humanly possible. Her eyes may look dull, her hair brittle, her skin stretched and taught over her bones. She does not, at this point, look even close to healthy or her former self.
- Cardiac problems occur in people with anorexia, at advanced stages. If she states she thinks her heart is racing or she is talking about signs that are common to heart attacks, she needs an ambulance right away.
- Hyperfocus on the eating habits of family members. She may become very insistent that you eat certain amounts of food that she prepares. She may even pressure you to eat and become insistent and irritable if you don't. This is the controlling part of her disease. Family members can feel like they are being forced to eat more than they want by their anorexic family member.

So what should you do if you or anyone who loves your daughter notices any of these signs or symptoms? The best step is to set up an appointment with her pediatrician. With eating disorders, it's imperative that she be evaluated from a health-status perspective. A care provider will likely want to run some blood tests to check electrolyte levels and other important chemistry profiles. You might talk with the pediatrician first about how he or she will share their concerns with your daughter. Talk to her mom, and don't back off on your concerns, no matter what anyone says, including your daughter, until you have medical clearance. Eating disorders are that important, that insidious, and provoke a lot of denial. If you face your fears and get them ruled out, hearing that she is okay from a trained medical expert is well worth the worry. If left untreated, these disorders can become the wildfire that started out as just a little leaf burning in your backyard.

Bullying

Sadly, the Youth Risk Behavior Surveillance (2009) found that 20 percent of students in the United States are bullied, despite the fact that many schools are increasingly aware of the ranges of behavior that fall under the category of bullying, as well as the ways that students are bullied—in person, in online social networks (Facebook, Myspace), via text messages or photos taken with cell phones, and more. The core behaviors of bullying are threats, marginalizing, and shunning. Many children don't tell an adult for a while, so they are left to fend for themselves for weeks or months. Bullying is not "kids will be kids." Students have killed themselves as a result of bullying. Students wait for the adults in the school setting, teachers and administration, to catch on, notice, and take action to protect them. However, that often doesn't happen. The bullying can be so covert that it's off the radar screen of the administration. Or teachers think that it's just "normal teasing." Dad, bullying is not normal or healthy and it can be devastating. If your daughter is the victim, consider these responses:

- *Listen.* Please be calm and listen a lot. If she sees you immediately respond in an aggressive way, she will stop talking. Understand she wants you to help, but she does not want to be seen as a cause of a problem. So this is the time to not react emotionally. Often bullying victims really need validation that what they have experienced is wrong. That's your best first response.
- Talk to your daughter about what she thinks is a good response strategy. This will give you an idea of what level of fear she has and what she's worried about if her concerns are known. Is she worried about even more bullying and retaliation? Does she want you to keep quiet because she doesn't think she can be kept safe in school? She is taking a risk asking for help, and she is also breaking the code of "don't tell on your peers." This is important.
- Log specific episodes of the event. This will likely mean access to her Facebook and e-mails, texts, etc. You should already be on her Facebook friends list, so this should not be hard. Get copies of e-mails and Facebook messages. Keep phone messages. Let her know that the more specific information you have, the better the response. You want to be taken seriously and logging events provides a clear event history. Be able to cite examples as specifically as you can.
- Talk to your daughter about the difference between asking for help and "telling on" someone. Support her bravery in asking for help. Appeal to her sense of right and wrong behaviors; helping those who are most vulnerable is a worthy behavior.

In our youth, bullying was taken in stride. It happened and we hoped to get out relatively unscathed. It occurred on sports teams, in school, even from teachers and coaches. We got it as students, from neighbors. The goal was to avoid the bully. It was seen as an unavoidable rite of passage of sorts. We were taught how to fight back or avoid, whichever would be more successful. Rarely did we think of engaging adults in our efforts to survive it. Often our parents, if they knew, were divided. Moms were concerned. Dads often said, "One good punch back and he'll stop bugging you." The conversations about bullying were not communitywide. Schools knew and often looked away for the most part. Some bullying behaviors in sports were simply seen as a normal way to establish a pecking order. We normalized it or looked away. General statistics suggest that up to 20 percent of kids are bullied with some frequency. Cyberbullying is most common in middle and high school (Youth Risk Behavior Surveillance).

Bullying is not a random event. When one person or a few together consistently pick on more vulnerable kids in ways that willfully hurt or harm, they are bullying. Bullies identify and isolate a girl who is less powerful. In girl-world, less powerful often means has fewer connections and is less "like the rest" in dress, weight, or height, or displays fewer things that suggest power like the right shoes, bags, or male attention. Bullies say and write hurtful things about their victim, with the intention of harming them socially or personally. They can often ruin or break personal belongings. Their goal is to elevate themselves by lowering their target's value, popularity. Their secondary gain is to show others what they can do to them if they challenge their position or power.

Thankfully, things have started to change in our overall understanding of types of bullying, but sadly it has taken teen suicides as a result of bullying to fuel that change engine. We no longer see bullying as par for the course, a developmental white water to be negotiated, sink or swim. School faculties and staffs are trained to spot and intervene. School policies are changing. Consequences for bullying can be quite significant including suspension and removal from sports teams and student groups.

However, we want to take a moment to remind you of how bullying most often occurs among girls. Books like Rosalind Wiseman's *Queen Bees and Wannabes* have started to flush out this behavior and are good sources if you want to learn more. Remember that one of the most important aspects of a female's life and sense of happiness is social connection. Her peer group's acceptance and inclusion is central to your daughter's happiness. That's why cliques are so powerful for tween and teen girls. So if your daughter begins to experience the type of bullying that is more common among girls, she'll be in significant discomfort. Her sense of herself is at risk if she is losing her social network. Let's take a minute to give an example of how this works, as we believe that female bullying is more finely tuned and subtle but as powerful as taking a punch from the center forward in the locker room.

Here's what a progressing bullying situation might look like. Your daughter has a good group of friends. She enjoys sleepovers, going to the mall with her group, and she feels quite comfortable socially. While in school, she starts to notice that her friends are not saving a place for her at the lunch table (step 1 in excluding her). This feels pretty awful for her; she feels left out, not important, not noticed. But she gives it time. Maybe she's misreading the situation. Maybe this will change. She doesn't talk to anyone about this.

Next, she notices that there are social events that she's not invited to. And she is painfully aware of this because all the invitations are being posted on Facebook. She can see who is going, who is getting invited, and the inside jokes about who isn't invited. She continues to feel more alone and marginalized. She starts to notice that there are some comments flying around on Facebook that let her know that she is farther from the group than ever. Comments are being made like, "Nobody wears those shoes anymore! Did you see her?" She feels awful. The conversations heat up with comments like, "Some people actually think that Rob might like them! Like that will happen! Can you imagine she thinks he'll ever like her?" No names, but clear understanding about who it's directed to. Other comments like, "Who would like someone who everyone knows is a whore?" and, "She'll do it with anyone! Why would that guy want to hang out with her?" start to appear online. None of this need be true. Once it's said out loud, it becomes truth even if there is no truth to any of it.

Photos taken on cell phones, bad photos, unflattering photos, photos of her laughing with her mouth full, taken unknowingly in the gym locker room, photos that your daughter never posed for are posted. Now anyone accessing that page can comment on these photos, and even tag them, forward them. She's now the victim of a local, viral Facebook page, and she may not even know it. But she's going to feel the social consequences.

This bullying now leaks over into the school setting. She hears very quiet comments and laughter as she walks down the hall. Sadly, this is a very specific and skillful style of bullying. And equally sadly, no adults catch wind. This is all happening off adult radar and it won't be noted until someone breaks the code and talks and asks for help. The girl who asks for help is a courageous and brave person. She is flying in the face of many norms. A girl has to see that this is cruel and bullying and go to an adult. The staff member who might slough it off or suggest that she just avoid those girls or that she not take it personally does not always note this type of bullying. That staff member cannot be the only adult who helps. Because this is bullying, and the girls who are doing it need to be held accountable. This behavior will continue and, like a virus, spread to the next vulnerable girl unless it is held up to the light and the girls are held accountable.

So what can you, as a dad, do when you hear about incidents like this? And what do you do when it's your daughter who is the victim or, perhaps, the bully?

Talk to other adults. And when you do, be prepared that you might not get support about this being bullying. We are far more familiar with male-based bullying. This style of bulling is sneakier, less direct, but clear. If a friend tells you it's not bullying, ask another. Ask a female who understands the female culture. Be aware that not every school official will agree with you. For any number of reasons, they may be uninformed or have their own bias. Don't hesitate to go up the line. Your daughter will likely have concerns that she will get some kickback about this, that someone will think she's stupid or isolate her. Don't let that happen. You must remain her ally and assure her that you will not tolerate any more bullying and that retribution would be more bullying. If your school officials are not supportive, bring the examples, and go in asking for a specific consequence.

In some cases, schools have in-house resource officers who are police officers assigned to the school to assist in taking care of students. If the bullying happens in cyberspace or outside of school, this person may be a great help to you and may be a bridge between the school response and a community response. You can often talk to them to get some ideas. Talking with them does not mean you are filing charges or anything of that sort. At times, alerting the parents of the bully and the bully herself that these are problematic behaviors is the additional help a parent needs.

Consider talking to the bully's parents. In many cases, a parent will be mortified that her daughter is engaging in this cruel behavior. In some cases, she will tell you you're wrong or that your daughter is no angel. That's not the issue. Stay on task with the information you have, the examples, and the outcome.

If your daughter or a friend of hers is affected, do not stop until action is taken and your daughter is no longer targeted. Be aware that even after the primary bully stops, her friends can carry on with the behavior, especially if that bully was punished. They now blame the victim for being the cause of the girl's suspension or being kicked off the hockey team. It has taken a great deal for this girl to talk to you about this. She is asking for your help. She is asking that something change. You, as her dad and her chosen adult, really need to step up and help, not convince her, not minimize, not ignore.

Now what if your daughter is doing the bullying? Pay attention. Listen to the concerns. Don't deny it, even if it's painful. People who bully are themselves feeling vulnerable; they just go about dealing with it in an offensive way. She needs some support, some clarity to her behaviors, some consequences. Bullying can easily get out of hand. Consequences will get bigger the older she gets. The last thing anyone wants is a teen to be held responsible for another's death due to bullying. So don't stick your head in the sand. Talk directly to your daughter. Don't ignore the evidence. Help her change now.

Texting and Sexting

We know that technology has made significant changes in our lives, some for the better and some that have brought new and unprecedented challenges to parents. With the help of cell phones, iPads, and computers, teens can be in almost-constant communication. This is not always a healthy thing. If we remember that a teen brain is a reactive brain, and then we hand it technologies that enable constant and immediate conversations, it's no wonder that texting and cyber communications are hotbeds of peer conflict, exclusion, and in some cases, dangerous activities like bullying and sexting. We cannot underestimate the lack of a time buffer with these technologies. Within seconds, an angry and mean text can be composed and sent out, an embarrassing naked photo can be posted, and then all bets are off. It's gone into cyberspace and on its way, like a worm to the core of an apple. When the immediacy of the Internet and technologies joins with an incredibly reactive teen brain, things can get out of control quickly.

Facebook and other social-networking sites can become extensions of clique behavior. In the old days, there were breaks in the day, meaning a student who was being bullied at school often had downtime at home, where there wasn't a constant and painful flow. When at home, they could regroup, talk to adults and parents, and get a break from the harassment. Now, with a cell phone, a computer, and some privacy at home, the bullying can continue 24/7 and take a larger toll on our kids.

So what should a dad do? Well, first, get educated. We know that the technology just doesn't stop developing, and our kids seem to be more on top of it than most of us. My daughter's favorite store is the local big-box electronics store. She loves going to see what the newest developments in laptops, accessories, and technology are. This was never an issue when we were growing up.

Phone calls came in to the house phone; our parents knew who was and wasn't calling. They knew when a conversation ended abruptly or when we were perched in the kitchen, waiting for the phone to ring. Technology has significantly changed this. So much of our children's lives can happen under the radar. However, there are things we can and should know in order to help keep our kids safe and balanced.

Text-Speak

Technology has brought with it its own language. Checking out our kids' conversations online can be like trying to read the court reporter's tapes during a trial; there are abbreviations and shortcuts that we just aren't familiar with. So how do we learn a new techno-language? Ironically, a few good websites are out there to help us, including www.noslang.com, www.netlingo.com, and www.lingo2word.com, which offers tech language translation. Some terms that any parent should know (and we understand that this language evolves, so staying current is key) include:

BF/GF	boyfriend/girlfriend
CD9	code 9 (parents around)
GNOC	get naked on camera
MOS	Mom over shoulder
NIFOC	naked in front of camera
P911	parent emergency
PAW	parents are watching
POS	parent over shoulder
PRON	porn
PRW	parents are watching
TDTM	talk dirty to me
WTF	what the fuck?

Some sexting terms you should know, because your child might know them, are:

8	oral sex
142	I love you
CU46	see you for sex
DUM	do you masturbate
GNRN	get naked right now
GYPO	get your pants off
IIT	is it tight?
IWS	I want sex

JO	jerk off
Q2C	quick to cum
RUH	are you horny?
YWS	you want sex

This is not an exhaustive list, but it surely shows how important it is for parents to be aware of the language, of where to find help in translating the language, and knowing what our kids are talking about, how they are talking to one another.

Drug and Alcohol Use

It's reasonable, given the climate and culture of our society today, to wonder if your daughter has ever had a drink or smoked a joint. Maybe you don't wonder; maybe you know for sure. American culture approaches underage drinking with a strict former-first-lady approach of "just say no." We don't want our kids to use illegal substances, but we put them on antidepressants at a frighteningly young age, give them their daily dose of stimulants following a cursory ADHD diagnosis, and then balk at a beer with dad after a round of golf when the teen is nineteen. Some parents support the view that "illegal is illegal" and think they hold a tight rein, and others smoke pot with their children.

Our European friends have different opinions. Frequently European children are introduced to alcohol at a relatively early age. Children in Italy and France often have small glasses of watered-down wine at dinner. And some of these European cultures have pretty low rates of alcoholism, while others have off-the-charts rates of addiction. So let's acknowledge the laws and consider how to approach your daughter if you have concerns.

The Youth Risk Behavior Surveillance conducted by the Centers for Disease Control in 2009 found that 42.9 percent of high school females had at least one drink of alcohol in the thirty days prior to the survey. That's almost half of the high school girls who, while underage, had a drink. Thirty-four percent smoked pot one or more times during their life. There are concerns that the most recent increase in use among teens are prescription drugs. With so much Adderall and other addictive stimulants being so heavily prescribed for ADD and ADHD, as well as pain medications available following a sports injury or surgery, it is no wonder that there is some sharing of these drugs going on. Both authors worked at a midsized university and repeatedly heard reports of students bringing whatever pills they had to a party, tossing them in a bowl, grinding them all up, and snorting the mix. That's scary. Taking a friend's medication is also common.

Unfortunately, the signs of alcohol or drug problems are some of the same signs of an eating disorder and depression. As a matter of fact, it's not uncommon for people to self-medicate their own depression or anxiety with alcohol or marijuana. If your daughter's grades are declining, she is missing or skipping school, her moods change and she's increasingly irritable or has crying jags, she has stopped participating in favorite activities, she starts becoming secretive by locking her bedroom doors, she has changed her group of friends and you don't know her new group, and if you find your money or valuables missing or if she suddenly has more money than she should, she might have some problems. If you find some drug paraphernalia in her jeans pocket, or a beer bottle under the car seat, do not pass go. Talk to her. She might have an excuse; she might blame you for going through her private stuff. Neither is the point. You're her parent and you have some evidence that you need to follow and not be derailed. Needless to say, if your child is charged with DUI, there is likely an alcohol or drug issue.

Again the mom-network you've established may be invaluable for you because when there are underage parties or someone shows up at a school mixer drunk, the grapevine of both kids and parents usually starts buzzing. If you are worried about possible use, notice her appearance, as she might be getting sloppy or coming home smelling like alcohol or pot. Her eyes may be dilated or bloodshot. Her hair and clothes might smell. These are things we know, but when it comes to noticing them in our daughters, we sometimes choose to look away. But you know what drunk looks like. Don't look away.

A single episode of pot use or drinking does not, on its own, suggest a problem. If she comes home high or drunk, talk to her when she is sober. The next morning we suggest a little reality therapy. Don't let her sleep late. Create a louder environment than she might prefer, and in short, help her be miserable as a result of her decision. A little aversion therapy may bring some points home so you don't have to. Let her feel the teeth of the dog that bit her.

Later in the day, sit her down and tell her, point blank, what you saw, what you believed happened, and what the consequences are. And there most certainly *should* be consequences. Tell her about your concerns. Ground her if you choose, but don't let that stop the conversation. Watch your liquor cabinet, talk to your ex and to your mom-network, and look for other signs.

If you see more, there are some screening tools that can pretty easily determine if someone has a drinking or drug problem. Connecting with a drug counselor who specializes in teens is a good idea. We can't state strongly enough that this professional has to have a good rapport with teens. Most teens will resist going to a counselor, but if the person does not know how to effectively be with teens, especially teen girls, in a way that does not alienate them, you will have wasted the cost of your co-pay and may find out no useful information.

If your daughter comes home drunk or is sent home from a school dance a second time, all bets are off, and you should contact a professional. A teen girl using substances to the point of intoxication is at significant risk for a number of bad outcomes. Most sexual assaults are date rapes, not stranger rapes. And the majority of them occur when one or both of the teens are under the influence. A drunken teen girl is less able to notice the signs of danger. Their inhibitions are lowered. People with lowered inhibitions do things like drinking and driving, going home with people they may or may not know well, and if they are depressed, attempting suicide. So there is a lot to look at here: at least risk reduction and maybe some level of intervention and treatment at the appropriate level.

Depression

We've long known that women experience depression at higher rates than men, most likely due to the constantly shifting hormonal levels. Depression in teens, however common, is not exactly easy to spot. Here's why. The symptoms are so common among teens (isolation, mood changes, increased crying or sadness, irritability, sleeping more or sleeping less, lack of interest and pleasure, difficulty concentrating). You can see that these symptoms sound like the teen years, so how can you differentiate whether or not your kiddo is depressed? Well, not easy, but here are some hints. If your daughter has a relative (mom, dad, grandparent, sibling, aunt, uncle, or cousin) who has had depression, it's worth watching for. There are strong suggestions that depression has a genetic component.

Maybe your daughter doesn't brighten up at all. She is constantly down with few breaks in her mood regardless of what's going on. She does not appear to have any periods of changed moods, no brightening when positive things happen, consistent lack of enjoyment.

Her sleep pattern is disrupted, but not because she is on the computer instant messaging all night. She's not sleeping because she can't sleep. Or she sleeps all day because she wants to avoid the world, not because she was up all night at a slumber party.

She might stop caring for her basic hygiene, or her attention to her appearance and cleanliness wanes. She doesn't care about her hair much anymore; she doesn't seem to care about what she looks like; she might not be brushing her teeth. Showers aren't important. And maybe she's crying a lot, for no known reason. You haven't heard her laugh at her favorite TV show in a long time.

The basic difference between what you see with depression and the more common moodiness of teenagers is the consistency coupled with behavioral change. And admittedly, even for a mental health professional this is not always an easy call. A full evaluation of depression should include not just a mental health screening, personal and family history review, and possibly some measure such as the Beck Depression Inventory, but also a comprehensive physical and some blood work. Diet deficiencies or an underfunctioning thyroid can mimic symptoms of depression. If there is a family history of thyroid problems, that should be noted in her chart and monitored.

There are many approaches to easing depression that are not medication-based. Increasing exercise, using meditation and mindfulness, challenging negative thoughts, and more can make significant dents in depression, so don't avoid getting her diagnosed out of fear that she'll have to take medication. The decision to start meds should not be taken lightly and should be proportional to the depth and severity of her symptoms. Some antidepressants are actually contraindicated for teens, as they actually can stimulate suicidal thoughts in teens rather than ease the depression. Regardless of the decision it should be made judiciously and in concert with her mother. A teen who has one parent who agrees to the med while the other does not, and maybe doesn't let her take it when she is with that parent, will not get any benefit from the medication and may end up feeling worse because of the inconsistent dosing. Don't get us wrong, medications are certainly a tool to consider in the fight against deepening depression, but they must be taken seriously. Many adults and teens respond well to CBT (cognitive behavioral therapy). It's certainly worth a try.

The sooner depression is identified and treated, the less likely that she will have a relapse or ongoing issues. But if low mood and helplessness persist, any of us is vulnerable to the effects of deepening depression, including suicide.

Suicide

The National Center for Health Statistics (*Health, United States, 2005*) ranks suicide as the fifth leading cause of death among children aged five to fourteen years old, and the third leading cause of death among those fifteen to twenty-four years old. In the United States, only motor vehicle accidents and homicides take more lives. In cold hard numbers, this means each year in the United States four thousand people aged fifteen to twenty-four die by suicide (American Foundation for Suicide Prevention [AFSP]). The AFSP states that American Indians and Alaskan youth are at highest risk, comprising 20 percent of the teen suicides, followed by white youth at 10.3 percent, Asian Americans at 8.5 percent, Hispanic youth at 7 percent, and African Americans at 6 percent. The Youth Risk Behavior Surveillance (2009) cites that 8.12 percent of high school females attempted suicide one or more times in the twelve months prior to taking the survey. And finally 70 percent of youth suicide attempters are frequent drug and alcohol users.

Many parents don't want to think that their child might be at risk for suicide, so we don't talk to them about it. Sometimes we don't even talk about it even when they want to start a conversation about it. There's a fear that if we mention it, it will put the idea in their head that was never there before, and suddenly they'll attempt it. That couldn't be farther from the truth. Talking to our kids, and being willing to learn the warning signs, to respond to signals, and to speak the word itself, are probably some of the healthiest steps we can take.

In general, females attempt suicide more often than males, but males complete suicide more often. When females attempt, they generally use pills or slower methods, giving them more time to change their mind and call for help. Males most often choose firearms; driving vehicles into trees, rocks, or into traffic; or hanging. All of these methods are impulsive and, sadly, highly lethal.

So let's get right to it and push through any discomfort and talk about signs and symptoms of suicidal behavior in teens.

1. *Threatening to kill herself.* If a teens says, "I'm going to kill myself," it's wise to stop right there and say, "Whoa. That's serious language and I'm going to take it seriously. Are you really considering killing yourself, or ending your life?" When you make it important, it means that you're listening. It also clearly tells your daughter that it's not a phrase you want thrown around and that you are going to stop and listen when you hear it. Importantly, do not be afraid to stop and look her in the eyes and ask, "Are you thinking of hurting yourself?" By asking her, you are not going to initiate a behavior. If you ignore her language, you may be missing a strong clue. If you ask directly, and she's not thinking of killing herself, she'll roll her eyes and say, "Oh please! Joking!" and then you can breathe again. If she is thinking about killing herself, she will feel like you're listening and that you're willing to hear more. That's when you can help.

2. *Talking or writing about death.* Teens often tend toward the dramatic, and if one writing assignment results in a poem about death, don't panic.

However, if there is a consistent theme of death, dying, or funerals in their art or writing, please pay attention.

3. *Dramatic mood changes.* These are sustained longer than the mood swings noted during the two to three days before a girl gets her period. In some cases, we see deep sadness lifting suddenly just before someone commits suicide. That seems to be the point at which she makes the decision, picks a method, a day, and feels a sort of relief that her pain will soon end.

4. *A sense of hopelessness,* verbalizations that they can't see that a situation or experience can ever change for the better.

5. *Isolation* from friends and family. She pulls back from friends, events, sports, fun that she used to have. She avoids connection.

6. *A previous or recent suicide among her friends, peer group, or school community.* One suicide among a group of teens plants the seed of possibility in other depressed or angry teens. Often they will see the huge outpouring of response—tears, flowers, and attention from the community—and see that as an appealing goal for themselves.

7. *If a family member has committed suicide, it raises the likelihood that another family member will also attempt or complete suicide.* It is not a guarantee, but when someone you love has opted to end their life, it puts it on the table as a solution. Often other family members attempt in either similar ways or at the same time of year.

8. *Giving things away.* The reasoning behind this is twofold. They won't need it anymore, and they want to control who gets what after they die. If your child starts doing this, take note and quick action.

9. *Any suicide rehearsal behaviors,* including writing notes and throwing them away or leaving them around, choosing clothing for her funeral, talking repeatedly about where she'd like to be buried or what she would like for a funeral.

10. *Increased substance use.* She might hide this from you, so watch for it. Watch for signs of alcohol use, pill use, pot smoking. Pay attention to her behaviors, your liquor cabinet, your medication bottles. Mood-altering drugs decrease inhibitions and increase impulsivity. This is a dangerous combination when a person is feeling hopeless and can't find options. Teens may make an impulsive decision they might not make otherwise.

Don't hesitate to be the parent who notices, who intervenes, or who is willing to ask, "Are you in so much pain that you are considering ending your life?" If you get a startling response of "Yes, I have," then breathe. You can call her pediatrician, school counselor, or therapist. Trust your own gut, even if others minimize your concern. If you saw smoke in your kitchen, you wouldn't call your friend and ask him what he thinks. You'd call the fire department and let them do what they know how to do. This is one of those times. Call a professional and ask for their help immediately. It is far safer to rule out suicidal depression than to be the parent who looks back on the signs and wishes they intervened.

Risk Factors for Suicide

Because teen brains do not yet have fully developed prefrontal cortexes (the part of the brain that slows down reactivity, that is willing to step back and review options, and the judgment/evaluative center of the brain), they often are vulnerable to spontaneous and reactive behaviors. Among teens, suicide is often a spontaneous and reactive behavior. Many teen suicides are in-the-moment reactions to problems they don't see solutions to. The sadness here is that almost all issues have solutions, but a teen mind can't necessarily conceptualize them. To top it off, a depressed brain has difficulty finding neutral or positive options. So even though a depressed person may be trying to solve a problem, it's not unlikely that their brain will offer suicide as a solution. The more hidden the thought of suicide, meaning the less the teen asks for help directly or indirectly, the more serious the situation.

One of the primary risk factors we know of is if a parent or sibling commits suicide. We have already talked a bit about the impact of a mother's decision to kill herself on her children. If a parent has committed suicide, it increases the risk level for her children to choose the same outcome. It's as if a parent has confirmed that suicide is an option. Even having family members who love you is not reason enough to stay alive. So if a mom, uncle, aunt, cousin, or grandparent has committed suicide, watch carefully for signs of depression and suicidal thinking or rehearsal behaviors. Rehearsal behaviors come in the form of writing suicide notes, research into methods on how to complete a suicide, overdose and then a call for help, cutting oneself or sitting with a gun, or picking out the music or flowers for a funeral.

When a teen commits suicide, we often see other teens in that community, school, or peer group make suicide attempts. Informed community members know this and watch for vulnerable teens in the community. All parents in that community need to do the same and not ignore their concerns.

Gay, lesbian, and bisexual teens are at risk for suicide when they consider the possible outcome of coming out to people they love, or if they are outed by someone else. Fear of rejection by family members and community increase the risk factors. If these teens have support from others, the risk reduces. Websites like www.itgetsbetter.org emerged following tragic suicides by young gay people. Fortunately the safety net around gay, lesbian, and questioning youth is growing and is more easily accessible online and through YouTube. Sadly, gay teens are still harassed, frightened, and isolated, fearing for their lives at times. Generally, strong connections with parents, teachers, coaches, mentors, instructors, group leaders, aunts/uncles, and others provide a protective factor.

As adults, we have to be aware of the stressors and risks in the lives of our daughters. If your daughter mentions killing herself, wanting to be dead, being "done," wanting to end her life, or other similar comments, it's important that you stop and take it seriously. We know that saying things like, "I just want to kill myself," is not an uncommon statement from teen girls. But how do you know the difference between a tough day and a suicide threat? Well, ask her. Here's an example of how to go about this.

DAD: So how was your day?

DAUGHTER: I just want to kill myself. I forgot my paper and turning it in late means I lost five points!

DAD: Five points makes you want to kill yourself? Really?

DAUGHTER: No, Dad. This is called a "figure of speech." I do not want to kill myself. I have thought about killing my teacher. I'm so overloaded with homework. I need your help to dig out of the load. Can you help me, Dad? I'm just overwhelmed.

DAD: I sure can. Let's problem solve for a minute. Want me to come in and you and I and your teacher can talk about you catching up?

DAUGHTER: Yup. But a banana split from Al's would ease the pain!

DAD: We're on it!

Or it could go like this:

DAD: Kiddo, you seem sad lately. Is everything okay?

DAUGHTER: I hate my life. I hate it. I wish I was dead. I'm done, Dad. I can't do this anymore. I have no friends and I suck at school. I hate my life.

DAD: Whoa. Those are really important feelings. Let's talk about this. What's up?

DAUGHTER: Nothing. I don't want to talk about it right now.

DAD: I know, honey. But I can't let this go. I love you and care about you and want to help you when life gets tough. I know some days really stink. But they pass. You've seemed so sad and withdrawn lately. What's the sadness about? And how can I help?

DAUGHTER: Don't you get it, Dad? There's nothing you can do. I hate my life. I just do.

DAD: I'm going out on a limb here, but you just mentioned you wished you were dead. That's a big statement. Is it true?

DAUGHTER: What do you mean?

DAD: Well, have you thought of how you would do it? Have you done any research on ways people kill themselves? (Dad should now be thinking, "Has there been any teen in the community—intimate or distant—that may be inspiring this thinking? Is there a family history of suicide? Have there been any recent losses like not making a team, breaking up with a boyfriend?")

DAUGHTER: Well, yeah, anyone can OD. Or that kid in the next town over hung himself.

From this brief conversation, this dad learned that this teen has thoughts of suicide, she has a lethal plan, and in this case, there is a peer suicide mentioned. Despite a strong desire to not go there, he stopped, took it seriously, and had a talk with his daughter. The next step is to not avoid her truth and to get her some help.

Too often we are afraid to talk about suicide, even when people mention it. We seem to fear that if we follow up someone's comment about suicide with a concerned inquiry, we will put a thought in their head that they may not have had before. With teens, we encourage you to think of them much the same way we thought about Hansel and Gretel. Teens drop hints, like a trail of breadcrumbs. The trail has a use and that is to find their way out of the forest. A teen who mentions suicide, killing themselves, ending their lives, being done with it all, wishing life was over, or more, wants someone to pull them aside and say, in a direct way, "Hey, I hear you and I love you enough to take you seriously, so we can get you help if you need it." There is no reason to believe that by mentioning suicide we cause anyone to say, "Oh I hadn't thought of that! What a great idea! Maybe I should try that!" Don't ever hesitate to ask. The worst thing that will happen is your teen will roll her eyes and say, "Dad! I was just kidding! Geesh. You really think I'd kill myself over that lame boy? Come on!"

Other signals that suggest that your child is at risk include:

- Marked downward changes in school performance
- Marked changes in social/peer behaviors and connections
- Increased isolation
- Increased use of substances, drinking
- Symptoms of depression
- Loss of interest in things that used to matter
- Difficulty sleeping
- Rehearsal behaviors like writing suicide or good-bye notes
- Researching suicide on the Internet, reading books or watching movies that focus on suicide, death, and funerals
- Giving away important possessions

Even thinking about suicide can be difficult for us. Just the fact that you read this chapter and didn't run from the topic says a lot about you. Remember, you don't have to, nor should you consider going it alone when you're worried about suicide and your daughter. Call a counselor, pediatrician, or clergyman. You can have ample support in addressing any concerns.

Abusive Relationships

Sadly, relationship abuse is on the rise among our teens. According to the Center for Disease Control's Youth Risk Behavior Surveillance (2009), 10 percent of high school students reported being slapped or physically hurt on purpose by their significant other. Many of us still want to believe that nobody we know, certainly not our daughters, has experienced this form of violence. In her book *Not to People Like Us*, Susan Weitzman graphically shows us otherwise, that domestic violence occurs in all socioeconomic classes and cultures.

Teens experience the same patterns and range of abuse as adults. The violence is usually multilayered, with stages of emotional violence coming first with name calling, degrading, and social isolation, followed by physical and/or sexual abuse. In teen girls, where self-esteem issues are so rampant, and connection is so important, an abuser has many potential victims who don't see the abuse coming. The challenge for parents, who have the ability to intervene and help their daughters disengage on a number of levels, is that the Internet and cell phones enable so much consistent communication that we may not be aware of but that are so instrumental to the abuser, that the pattern may be in place and the abuse occurring for some time without our knowing. Abusers engage in controlling their victims. So the ability to text incessantly and to follow her moves on Facebook is far easier than it should be. However, there are things you as a parent can do to help prevent your daughter from becoming a victim.

- Meet, face to face, the group of teens she hangs out with. If she's dating, have her date come pick her up and sit with you for a while. Have him over for dinner, or to watch a movie with you. Do this several times. You'll notice something that might put the hair up on the back of your next. How he jokes with her, what he says about the guy in the movie who shouldn't let his girlfriend do that, etc. Don't encourage your daughter to meet him at the mall for the movie. Make him come and see you, repeatedly. You need to watch how he interacts with her and others. Knowing that people can put on great fronts to impress fathers, go to his lacrosse games, meet his parents—no matter how embarrassing that sounds to your daughter. You are looking for a few things, primarily how he manages frustration and anger. Is he repeatedly tossed out of the game for roughness despite penalties and his coach talking to him? Do his parents interact aggressively and abusively with you, with him, with the coaches?
- Institute tech breaks at home, where everyone turns in their phones or turns them off (like at night after 10 p.m.) and steps away from their computers. If your daughter is being cyberharassed by this boy, she will be nervous because he will get angry if she does not answer a text or page. Besides, time away from the Internet is a good thing. Frequently these abusers will text girls hundreds of times during the day, wondering where they are, who they are with, what they are doing, wearing, thinking. It's not a loving-crush kind of fascination. It's over the top, bothersome, and anger-based. If you're watching you'll probably notice that when she gets text messages she shows signs of anger, fear, or frustration. She wants a break from this and can't get it. If you have access to her phone, you may think about reading some of these texts, or if you see that there is an extraordinary amount of texting from and to a single number, you may want to look deeper into this.
- She will be nervous about being late, what she's wearing, and where she's going, not in the usual teen girl "how do I look" way. The abusers often try to control what girls wear, pressing them to wear clothes that either are too sexy for their tastes and they feel awkward, or are plain and cover her body. Along with her mind, he wants to control her body and her sexual attractiveness. You might hear her say, "David doesn't like it when I wear makeup," when you know she likes to use a little mascara.

- She might start doing poorly in school. This is taking up her time, as well as her energy. She is feeling frightened from moment to moment. What if he calls and she's not there? What if he's angry that she went to the movies with her girl friends? Many abusers stalk and show up at places where they know they will "catch" their victims. This adds to the sense of being under his control.
- If there is pushing, shoving, hitting, he will blame her, saying that she incited him so much he had to hit her, or he will be so remorseful and even tearful, promise that it will never happen again, and possibly shower her with gifts immediately following the event. The problem is that it's very likely that it will happen again and again, and if she doesn't walk out of the relationship the first time it happens, it gets increasingly harder for her to leave.
- Often the abuser threatens to kill himself and tells her it will be her fault if he does. These threats usually emerge when the girl makes moves to end the relationship.

The abuser's profile tends to include the use of alcohol or drugs, the inability to manage his anger and frustration in many settings (that's why you want to watch him at a game or with his friends), witnessing domestic violence in his own home, and having low self-esteem, but you won't notice that unless you know him well. He blames others more often than seeing his role in any experience. He may be quite charming and successful, or he may be struggling and an outcast.

As a dad, you play a very important role in helping identify this in a partner. Your daughter likely trusts you and hopes you will help stop this abuse. She will be embarrassed and worry what will happen if anyone finds out, but your role is to be her clear-thinking rock and to be very helpful in getting this to stop. Every moment she listens to this boy, fears him, changes her behaviors to please him, she believes what he says about her being worthless, fat, ugly, stupid, lucky to have him because nobody else could ever love her, and on and on.

This, like sex, drugs and alcohol, and money management, should be a topic that you and she talk about long before you're concerned about her relationship. Whenever possible, remind her how a healthy stable guy acts on good days and when he's frustrated. When she hears you, Dad, tell her that at no time should a woman ever be hit, demeaned, threatened, controlled, or abused, it will mean a lot. The more she hears it, in as many ways as possible (as a comment about a scene in a movie, a book you're reading, a new story, or what you heard about another teen via the mom-network), the more she'll believe what you say and turn to you for help, because you've repeatedly said,

"If this ever happens to you, please come to me. I'll help you. I won't judge you. You're my daughter. I'm here."

Sexual Assault

Although sexual assault has been previously mentioned, it is again worth noting in the section on concerns. As tweens and teens develop, they become increasingly vulnerable to sexual assaults. Girls between sixteen and twenty-four years old have the highest rates of rape and sexual assault (Baum et al. 2009). Nearly one in three sexually active teen girls in grades 9–12 (32 percent) report physical or sexual violence at the hands of their dating partners (Decker, Silverman, and Raj 2005). In general, more than 70 percent of rape victims know their attackers ("Rape and Sexual Violence"). So preparing our daughters to prevent stranger rape is less effective than talking with them about date rape, which often happens on a date but can also happen at a party, after a sporting event, or on a school overnight field trip. The term *date rape* can misrepresent it, but it reminds us that there are, among us, people who will take advantage of our daughters.

When a friend or person who we know, and probably have some level of comfort with, assaults a woman, it's not often interpreted as rape. How could a friend do such harm? They looked like a friend, talked like a friend, and behaved like a friend for a while. Approximately 48 percent of women who met the criteria for sexual attacks did not consider what happened as rape ("Rape and Sexual Violence"). This astounding statistic suggests that sexual assault is not easy to come to terms with, let alone confide in someone else about. The victim continues to be held accountable or bear the brunt of the legal process.

If your daughter tells you she's been assaulted, remember, for a daughter to tell her father anything about her sexual experiences is pretty unusual. To tell a father about an assault is incredibly difficult and likely suggests a high level of discomfort on her part. The myth continues, promoted in the media, that women either cry wolf about being assaulted or cry rape when she has had sex she regrets. This is a highly unlikely situation and a person who would accuse someone of such a level of crime without cause is likely to be deeply disturbed. And honestly, if you had a teen daughter who was struggling this much with her internal emotional world, you would likely have seen other signs and symptoms of unusual behavior. Remember, girls strive to be connected. Girls who falsely accuse boys are ostracized. Heck, girls who report a sexual assault are likely to get ostracized to some extent. So if your daughter discloses that she thinks she was sexually assaulted, there is enough reason to believe her.

If the person who assaults your daughter is someone she knew, it is often a boy who she has spoken with, hung out with, or even had a crush on. They could be on a date and the date goes horribly wrong. The key to understanding this type of assault rests in understanding the confusion on the part of the girl. Yes she may have agreed to and looked forward to the date. Yes she may have agreed to kiss or touch. Yes she may have really liked this guy. Yet when it comes to sexual assault, she did not agree. She did not consent and she did not want it. Even if she did consent but then communicated that she wanted to stop, either with words or actions (trying to leave the bed, saying, "No," or, "Stop," or, "I can't do this," etc.), and the boy did not stop, that is sexual assault.

Consent is the center point of legal sexual encounters. In this age group, consent is often forced or coerced out of a girl by drugging the victim or getting her to drink so her defenses are down. Importantly, people who are under the influence of alcohol or drugs that alter their mind or consciousness cannot give consent. So if a girl is fed beer, or has had some alcohol, legally she cannot give consent. If a boy intentionally feeds her drugs or alcohol, he can be charged with aggravated sexual assault as well as providing liquor to a minor and more. This holds true for our daughters who are in college. Until your daughter is of legal drinking age, it should be considered that she may have been set up to drink or had some drug dropped in her beer that facilitated the assault.

If a date-rape drug was dropped in her drink, she will find it difficult to remember any details. Date-rape victims often remember the early part of an evening, they can often remember putting their drink down or leaving it somewhere, and then there is often some faint memory of feeling ill, uneasy, or unusually queasy. The next thing that happens is she ends up somewhere with no memory of getting there (like back at her house or in a bedroom). She may be naked or partially dressed. She has a sense of something going wrong but cannot put her finger on it. These girls often feel ill, not hungover. They are slightly disoriented and just have a sense that something bad has happened, with very few specific memory traces. Importantly, if a girl feels this way, take her to a doctor and have her tested because date-rape drugs are only detectable for less than thirty-six hours.

Sexual assault carries potential physical side effects of sexually transmitted infections, injury to the pelvic or anal area, and potential unwanted pregnancy. Psychologically it leaves different scars such as sexual dysfunction, depression, PTSD, and more. The sooner she accesses a helper who she trusts and who knows how to treat assault victims, the sooner she can begin to heal. Most emergency rooms have nurses who are trained in the SANE (sexual assault nurse examiner) method of responding to sexual assault, where the care of the victim is the primary focus, even when gathering forensic evidence. Ask your healthcare providers if they are trained in SANE methods and approaches to victims. How others respond to your daughter is important. If someone blames her or minimizes her experience she may not seek help. As her dad, do everything you can to help your daughter as soon as possible. Support her if she wants to file a report to police or campus security. Reassure her that you believe her, and be her advocate. Remind her that she is safe. Sexual assault, especially date rape, has the potential to alter her whole worldview. What was once a safe world may now seem unsafe. She needs help on many levels to get through this. Her resources will help her, and you are certainly one of her primary resources.

And, suffice it to say, if this happens to any of our daughters, we go through our own emotional range from anger to fear to sadness for our children. Add some helplessness, a bit of retribution seeking, and confusion, and you've just scratched the surface of what a parent experiences. Don't forget to get some help and support for yourself. This is one of the most difficult experiences a parent can endure. To help your daughter, you likely need some help and support. Take care of yourself so you can take care of her. She needs you.

Unplanned Pregnancy and Options

Hearing your daughter tell you that she thinks she might be pregnant is likely to be one of those moments that stops your heart for a minute. In some cases, your daughter may first tell her mother, but not always. When raising a child, very little is relegated to just one parent, so we want to include you in the conversation about teen pregnancy.

The alarming statistics gathered by the Guttmacher Institute (2011) reveal that one in five (19 percent) of teen females who are at risk of unplanned pregnancy (those having intercourse) are not using contraceptives. The United States continues to have one of the highest rates of unplanned teen pregnancies in the developed world. Although the rate of teen sex is similar to that in Europe and other similar countries, our teens have more sex outside of committed relationships, leading to less discussion between partners about contraceptive use and less actual use of contraceptives. Among U.S. teens, 13 percent had intercourse before the age of fifteen and by the age of nineteen, seven in ten teens have had intercourse (www .guttmacher.org/pubs/FB-teen-sex-ed). Of the approximately 750,000 teen pregnancies that occur each year, 59 percent will be carried to term and result in a live birth, 14 percent will end naturally in miscarriage, and 27 percent will end in elective termination, or abortion.

If your daughter becomes pregnant, she will need a great deal of support. Too many parents choose that time, when she is considering the impact of being accidentally pregnant, to deride and punish her for being sexual or for forgetting to use contraceptives. This is simply not the time to do that. Much is at stake during the early weeks of a pregnancy, all of which will have a potentially long-term impact on whatever outcome she chooses.

Too often teens deny the signs of pregnancy and are in such denial that they might be pregnant that they don't take a pregnancy test immediately after missing a period, which is unfortunate. Early home pregnancy tests, available at every drug store for a relatively inexpensive price ($10 to $25), are as accurate when used as directed as many blood tests. In these early weeks, much is on the line. If she is considering maintaining the pregnancy, good nutrition, prenatal vitamins, and health-forward behaviors are central to the development of a healthy fetus. If she is considering terminating the pregnancy, it is a much easier procedure if done as early as possible.

After confirming a pregnancy, she has three choices. She can terminate the pregnancy and, as mentioned, with this option time is of the essence. She can choose to carry the pregnancy to term and keep the baby. Or she can carry the pregnancy to term and relinquish the baby for adoption. In making these choices, she will be faced with some very heavy-duty questions of what is best for her own future, how developed and available are resources if she chooses to keep the baby, and how she might handle relinquishing a child to a person or couple she may or may not know. This is a moment that calls for all the possible maturity and balanced thinking that she can muster in herself and from those who love her. It is a most emotional moment, and if you can be calm, honest with her in helping her review her options, and support her, you will make a difference. This is not the time for lectures. The horse is out of the barn and everyone knows it, and the goal is to act now, review errors in decisions later.

Let's talk about the time frame. The passage of time is most relevant to the girl who is considering an abortion, the reason being time impacts choice of method (suction versus mefipristone/misoprostol pills). The medications are able to stop the growth of cells and then cause the uterus to empty itself, and in that way mimics a miscarriage. The teen can go through most of this at home, and the process will take just a few days. There is no surgery necessary, but she must meet with a clinician for an initial visit as well as a follow-up visit. The pill process can be used up to nine weeks into the pregnancy (or sixty-three days from the first day of her last period). With teens, this matters because some teens don't keep accurate track of their menstrual cycle, so they might not know if they fall into the eligibility range. If she waits to take a pregnancy test until she misses two periods, she might see the window on this approach close. This process is more than 97 percent effective in terminating a pregnancy. The follow-up evaluation assures that all contents of the uterus have been released. If this is not true, a suction abortion is the recommended approach. This, too, is an outpatient process.

The other option is suction abortion, usually done from five to fifteen weeks gestation. The procedure itself takes about ten minutes, with recovery time being a few hours of observation. In some cases, the patient spends most of the day at the clinic, especially if the pregnancy is between twelve to fifteen weeks along. Suction abortions are approximately 99 percent effective (Planned Parenthood of Northern New England). Most clinics offer a range of anesthetics both to sedate the woman during the procedure and to offer some pain coverage. There will likely be cramping, and the providers may send the woman home with additional pain medication. In some clinics, pre-abortion counseling is offered or required. It's not a bad idea. The decision to terminate a pregnancy, even when it seems like the best option, is not an easy one to make, and some thoughtful consideration will likely help the person understand that she did consider the options thoroughly.

Abortion laws vary from state to state. Texas and Utah mandate that a parent sign permission papers to allow the teen to have an abortion. Some think that this somehow ensures that parents will support their children one way or another after learning of the pregnancy. Others fear that it prevents teens who have complex relationships with their parents, or, in some cases, who are being abused by parents, from getting the care they want. If your daughter is considering a termination, she will likely learn of the specifics of her state and may approach you out of need and with some fear.

The father of the pregnancy currently has few rights. General wisdom suggests that just as it was the responsibility of the mother to use contraceptives, so too it was the responsibility and right of the boy to insist on wearing a condom. Some girls want the father involved in the conversation and others never tell him. Unless there is a specific legal issue in your state, the decision lies with your daughter.

If she opts to maintain the pregnancy, she should have immediate medical care. Diet and vitamins are essential to delivering a healthy child. There are several avenues to relinquishing a child. Private (often arranged through a lawyer) versus agency adoption, open (the adoptive parents agree to keep the biological mother informed of the child's growth and progress, and some include the possibility for levels of future contact) versus closed (the baby is relinquished with legal agreements that there will be no contact between the mother and the new nurturing family and the child). Once a teen opts to keep the pregnancy, she has time to consider whether she will raise it or relinquish it. However, what seems like a long time, nine months, passes quickly when such important decisions are in the air.

Socially, this teen is at risk of isolation if her school suggests she now become homeschooled or if her friends reject her. She is also at risk of becoming idealized by her peers who think this is a great thing, and they offer shallow support in her decision to keep the child. The truth is, most teens need far more than good friends to raise a child. Most teens will be single parents with all the stresses that situation has the potential to bring. This is why a parent or other adult with insight, care, and calm is one of the best resources for this teen. She must figure out if she is really ready to put off her goals and be a mother and if she has the emotional and financial resources to raise a child.

As hard as this may be, if you can stand by her and offer unbiased considerations for options, she will have the best chance of adjusting to the new life ahead of her or to her decision to terminate. Neither is easy. Neither is optimal. Neither is over once the decision is made. A parent should remember that many women and teens have decided to terminate and go on to live wonderful lives, achieve their dreams, and decide later if they would like to become pregnant again. There is no medical evidence that suggests that future fertility is impacted by a clinical abortion. Likewise, women have made the decision to relinquish into an adoptive family.

Her decision will also likely have an emotional impact on you. You will wonder if she'll be okay. You'll wonder about the "what ifs" of her decision. You will remember her due date and find yourself noting it when it comes around, and you'll note the date of the birth if it happens. This is a normal and natural response. There is grief. So if you find yourself feeling that sadness and want to talk it through, please don't hesitate. Every dad and every mom wants to protect their child from pain and fear. We have not failed simply because our children go through things we wish they wouldn't. Perhaps we only fail if we stop being their loving parents as they go through the experience. This is a difficult one. Take care of her and take care of yourself.

One more quick thing to think about. Do not assume that your teen will get on the pill or always use contraception because she had an unplanned pregnancy. Follow through with her gently and respectfully, offering to support her if she needs a ride to the doctor or wants to get shots or use other types of prevention. Teen brains, as you recall, are not fully developed until they are in their early twenties. They can kick back into denial and a sense of "that couldn't possibly happen again." Don't be afraid to continue your support of her life and her future.

For more information on the processes, options, or the laws in your state, you can find resources listed in the bibliography at the back of this book.

CHAPTER
10

Being a Great Dad

First Things First: Becoming Spider Dad, or Why Networks Are Important

One of the keys of being a successful single dad is to develop and strengthen a new network. Women and girls are wired for connection, literally. In her book *The Female Brain* (2006), Louann Brizendine, M.D., reminds us that the parts of the brain that serve relationship-building and connection are actually larger in women than in men. We build spiderwebs of contacts with teachers, physicians, guidance counselors, coaches, and daycare providers. Our peer group behaviors are largely about that, connection. That is why we can sit over coffee and talk for two hours and walk away with everything but their social security number. Through conversation and connection, women build trust and cooperation with others who are willing to help us because they feel they know us. If you understand the importance of these connections for both you and your daughter, you'll find adjusting to the changes of single parenthood much easier. To put it simply, as a single dad, you need to be "one of the mothers": when in Rome do as the Romans do.

As women are chatting at the sidelines, at bake sales, or in the after-school pick-up line, we are doing far more than laughing and smiling. We are connecting. In order to connect, we share information that proves we trust one another, such as who might not be a good babysitter, and we talk about couch colors, new jobs, and "Oh, by the way—can you drive my daughter to the soccer game this weekend and I'll take them to the after-game party? Oh, you didn't know about that? Yeah, there's a party and a carwash next weekend. Did you hear that one of the kids in school got caught with steroids?"

Not only are we sharing information that is important to our children's well-being, but we are also becoming logistically important to one another and personally vulnerable, which shows that we trust one another. It's a dance. Info, personal revealing, support; again, info, personal revealing, support. Over and over, quietly we dance this dance. The more we do this, the more we trust one another and the more likely we are to help one another and our children. We depend on one another. Those women we chat with are the same moms we trust enough to be on our emergency contact lists at school. They may be the moms who offer to watch the kids on a snow day when we have to go to work. Together we have chaperoned field trips and comforted each other's daughters when they missed making the goal and cried all the way home. We know that we're all wondering about aging and are afraid for our 401Ks and that we think our best friend might have a drinking problem. We generally don't trust those who don't reveal something about themselves.

These are integral members of the village that it takes to raise our children. And because they are women with daughters, they will be invaluable resources to you as you raise your daughter.

Men generally connect with each other through activity. Maybe you remember a conversation with your ex, or a date, following your Sunday golf game. You were enjoying a plate of nachos and she leaned over and asked you, "Hey, what did John say today about Mike and Martha's separation?" You looked at her with a quizzical expression and replied, "Margie, we golfed. We talked about putters, balls, angles, types of grass, new drivers, and what to have for lunch. Then after breaking for a burger, we golfed and talked about putters, balls, shot angles, types of grass, new drivers, and when to stop for beer." She looked at you, shocked, and asked, "How could any four friends spend five hours together and not talk about personal stuff?" Well, easily if the group is four men. Connection is different. It comes through parallel experiences, activity, and gentle or not gentle competition. You engage in side-by-side activities, with some level of pecking order. If you try to do it this way, with a bunch of mothers at a soccer game, or on a field trip, you won't be let in, and if you're on the outside of some networks, that could have some real consequences for how effectively you single-parent.

As a single dad, you might be spending far more time in direct care of your daughter than many of your male friends or neighbors. It will really help if you integrate yourself into the networks that are central to your daughter's activities and the groups of parents who support those activities. It will make your life much more manageable if you know her friends' mothers and fathers. Up to this point, if you've been less involved in your daughter's life than your wife was, you may be an unknown entity. Or if your daughter is a teen and you are less familiar with her friends, as is often the case for both moms and dads, you may need to do some catch-up work. Become a part of the carpool rotation. Make a point of talking to parents at games. Volunteer to chaperone field trips or dances. Host a team breakfast at your home. In short, act like many moms do. By doing this, you are connecting with the moms and dads, increasing their trust in you, and increasing the likelihood that you will come to mutually support your children.

In just the same way, make direct contact with your daughter's teachers. Send an introductory e-mail saying, "Hi, I'm Jennifer's dad and just want you to know how to reach me if you need to. She's with me on Monday, Tuesday, and Wednesday night of each week, and I really want to know if there are any homework issues or concerns. Hearing good things is wonderful, too." Know when parent-teacher conferences are and attend them. Call the school nurse to say, "Hi. If Jen's ever sick or you have any health concerns, please call me or my office at this number." If you contact the school nurse or the coach to let them know you're Amy's dad and you want to be sure she's doing okay in school because she had a sore throat when she woke up today, that word will spread among other moms. You will earn street credibility for caring, active engagement, and connecting. Similarly, if you send your child to school without a permission slip time after time, or unprepared to an away game, you're credibility will suffer with each oversight, just as it does when a mom seems to have her head somewhere else. That's why it's like a spiderweb. One bit of damage on one side of the web will resonate and threaten the entire web. One effort to strengthen the web on one side strengthens and spreads goodwill across entire web.

You may have noticed we used the word *trust* because, and don't shoot the messenger please, single fathers are sometimes stereotyped and assumed to be less engaged and less reliable as far as children go. Tradition holds that the mother is the "present" parent, especially for tween and teen girls at school and social and sports events. Dads show up for games, moms carpool to and from practices, rehearsals, and school concerts. We simply see moms more, so we know them more, and so we trust them more. Add the fact that you're a single guy who might start spending a fair amount of time with moms, and rest assured trust is important. If you are connecting with a group of moms, make a deliberate effort to connect with their partners as well. A single male in a group of moms can easily and erroneously be seen as "trolling the waters" so always acknowledge and respect their partners and their marriage/relationship. Go out of your way to not be flirtatious. A flirty single man will not be trusted and therefore will not be allowed into the network. Finally, and sadly, a flirty single dad, depending on the age of the daughters, can be seen as a threat to girls' safety as well. We have heard the stories of the dads who have affairs with the college-age nannies, babysitters, the daughter in another family. Similarly, we all know about the "good dad" who baked the cookies for the soccer party, who volunteered to chaperone the dance, and who bravely spent long hours helping build the set for last year's theater production.

Single men raising daughters should, on some level, borrow the attributes of good mothering. Here are the basic tenants:

- Be there.
- Show up and be useful. Pitch in.
- Contribute to the work of the day, whatever it is.
- Donate time, energy, and food.
- Be generous with what you can contribute like carpooling, hosting celebrations, and organizational skills for the team carwash, bottle drive, or fund-raiser.
- Be reliable. If you say you'll do it, do it. If you commit to being there, be there.

Again, when in Rome, do as the Romans do. The best way to be a successfully networked single dad is to follow the lead of networked mothers. Blend in. It will work for you.

Watching You Now More Than Ever

Ever feel like you're being watched? Stalked? Observed like some kind of rat in a cage? Well, good, because you are. Your daughter is watching you from many angles. She learns more from watching you than she does from listening to you. And since there's just one adult in your home, you have her undivided attention. She's watching you for cues about how she can handle the change. She's watching you now because up until the divorce or death, you were part of the package deal called "momanddad." She's learning about you in a more direct way, without Mom around, learning about you through her own lens. This is an important aspect of her adjusting to the new situation.

Here's just a short list of things she's learning about you:

- *How you talk about and treat women.* Any women. The women in the grocery, the women behind the counter at the store, her lacrosse coach. Her teachers. Her best friend's mom. She's listening to what you say to them face to face, and how you say it, and she's listening to what you say about them in the car.

- *How you deal with your money*. How you use it, how you direct it, and what sort of access she has to it. She'll notice if you use money to substitute for other forms of love and caring.

- *How you drive*. Yes. If she's a tween or teen thinking about getting her own license, she's watching you and the speed limit, you and safety, comments you make about speed traps and more. I could tell when my daughter started to think about her own driving because it was as if I now had a driver's education teacher riding shotgun. "You pulled out a little quickly there, Mom." "You know you're going ten miles over the speed limit here, Mom." And as surely as I'm glad she delights in reminding me of the rules of the road, I realized that I was also modeling her next big adventure, driving. She was learning by watching. That's when I started driving a bit better . . . when she's with me.

- *How you manage conflict and stress*. She'll notice if you have a bad day and don't talk to her, or if you sputter about what an idiot your boss is, or how angry you are at Congress. The way you do it is as much a teaching tool to her as what you are saying. So if you want to teach your daughter some life skills, do it by talking about your day, how you approached some conflict, how you thought it through, and how it worked. Let her know when you make mistakes! Let her know that people she loves and respects goof up and repair.

- *Dating*. Boy, oh boy is she watching you—how you select women, how you treat them, and what you say about them. Her eyes will be on you like a dog on a bone. And in this case, you will want to teach her what you want her to expect, if not demand, from a boyfriend/partner when she's old enough. Should she expect to be treated respectfully or will she watch you go from woman to woman, each of whom meets her over cereal on Saturday morning, and learn to follow in your footsteps?

- *Drinking and drug-use habits*. She listens hard for what you say about alcohol and drugs. If you walk in the door after a hard day and say, "Boy, do I need a martini!" guess what she'll say sooner than later? The harder part, and the part that's open for discussion in the field of child development, is how to answer the question, "Dad, did you ever use drugs?" There is no perfect answer to that, except be really careful to not say, "Hell yeah, and it was the best decision I ever made!" Other than that, you'll have to figure this one out on your own. When I get questions like this, I wonder, what's the question she's really asking? Could she be asking, "Should I smoke with those kids at that party next week?" or is she asking your permission and support to say "no"? I always tell my daughter that I am her big bad wolf. If she gets asked or urged to do things that morally, ethically, or internally set off alarms, use me. Tell them, "If I do this, my mother will kill me where I stand." It gives her a route out, without having to directly push back against peer pressure. She may well be asking for your decision-making process in similar circumstances. Don't look like a perfect white knight. "No, honey, I was never tempted to drink beer." Instead say, "Yeah, it was a tough decision. I thought about getting home to my dad and looking him in the eye; I thought about getting caught and how that would affect my place on the team, and I realized it was just not the decision I wanted to make at that time." That's an honest, careful, exposed response. She can learn a lot about you and about decision making in that response. And she will learn that she can ask you that and you won't jump down her throat for asking for your insight, because that's what she's doing. And you should feel honored. She trusts you enough and she respects you enough to want to know about you.

- *Are you trustworthy?* Do you have integrity and honesty? Do you follow through on your commitments, even if they are difficult? Do you pick her up when you say you will? Do you show up for games? Do you call when you say you'll call? Do you hold that boundary, or do you cave in when she cries? You promised her a sleepover for her birthday. If you cancel that, unless you are bleeding out in the emergency room somewhere, she's learning more about you than you ever intended to show her. Are you able to set limits and keep them? If you say, "No, you can't sleep over at your boyfriend's house," do you uphold it even when she's crying and telling you she hates you? Because she's watching.

- *Are you engaged in your community?* Do you drop a can of soup in the donation box at the grocery store? Do you encourage making and keeping commitments to school activities, neighbors, your temple or church, even when the weather is so good all you want to do is play golf that morning?

- *How you manage anger or other challenging emotions.* If you're able to cry in front of her when your parents die, or if you're able to say you're angry without throwing things, accusing someone else, or getting drunk, then you're teaching her good emotional skills. It's really wise to put it out there. Children, especially girls, are sensitive to emotional states. If you're angry, say it. If she senses it but doesn't know why, she'll try to figure it out, and that often includes assuming responsibility on her end, which is often not true. So it's much healthier to say, "I'm really angry at Uncle Bob. We've had a disagreement that we haven't settled yet. I'm going to go hit a bucket of balls to let off a little steam." Then she'll have a context, a reality check, and be able to not assume that she is at the center of your frustration or anger.

Most daughters love their dads. Some don't. If your daughter loves and respects you, you will become her template for future men in her life. If you teach her what is healthy, respectful, and loving behavior, she'll move toward that in her own life. You teach her, every day, either by example or by default. Daughters of fathers who cheat on their partners learn to expect cheating. Daughters who watch their fathers be abusive learn to accept abuse. Daughters who learn that they can take their dads for a ride will learn to manipulate and disrespect their husbands.

The truth is, daughters tug at fathers' hearts in a unique way. So many dads have told us when they first held their infant daughter, they felt completely helpless to say no and completely prepared to give them the world. Mothers tend to think things like, "I will teach you to be strong, loving, and smart." One dad said, "The minute I held her, all I wanted to do was give her everything she wanted. I was ready to hand over my heart and my credit cards at that moment." What she really needs is not a golden ticket and a thick wallet, but rather constant support, insight, love, and caring. You are her role model. Do you hope, one day, that she says, "Dad, I want to marry a man just like you?" Be that man.

On the Lighter Side: "Dad, I Want to Have a Party!"

Being able to host the social life of your daughter will win you more points. If you're a good party thrower, then carry on. It's a rare gift. The truth is, girls like parties. Some like big ones, some small ones, and they don't have to fall on a certain occasion. If your daughter has an event coming up, a birthday, graduation, honors society event, regional hockey finals, etc., feel free to stage a celebration. The key to a good girl party is to let your daughter pick a theme (yep, they like theme parties for the most part, overt and subtle) or tell you what she wants, because she knows her peers best. Then you do your best to make some iteration of that happen. It's just that simple. Note: *Do not feel compelled to spend a lot of money.* Some parties have gotten so big, commercial, and so out of hand it can put pressure on the rest of us parents to rent out the room at the club, hire a DJ and a light show, and throw a full buffet for our kid's birthday. Must we? If we do that for a fourteen-year-old's birthday, what will we do for their graduation? We're big believers in the following approaches to parties:

- Listen to your daughter's overall idea.
- Have lots of food (think nachos, chips, veggies and dips, a bowl of M&M's is necessary, milkshakes, do-it-yourself sundaes and pizza).
- Have music and movies (especially if it's a movie-theme night).
- Consider some sort of make-it-yourself sundae bar, popcorn-topping option, decorate-your-own-cupcake approach.
- Give them a room and let them spread their sleeping bags and stuff, lots of stuff, out.
- Leave them alone, almost. You have to pop in occasionally.
- Have a backup goofy thing, like balloons for water balloons, weirdly colored nail polish and remover, facemasks and stuff for quick facials.

We just heard of a blast of a party that the fifteen-year-olds loved, where the dad, creative guy that he was, went on the Internet and searched for "facials you can make in your kitchen" recipes. He bought mangos, plain yogurt, cucumbers, oatmeal, olive oil, and some other inexpensive stuff. He printed off the recipes for the do-it-yourself facials and the girls had an incredible night, making their own masks and washes and moisturizers. Not much cost and from the word on the street, this dad is a party king!

Anyway, your daughter has a wonderful idea cooking somewhere about her party. Maybe just a pizza, movie, and nail polish party. Maybe an end-of-the-year photo-collage-box-making event for the basketball team. Maybe karaoke. Maybe it's theme movie night, like Twilight all-night, Harry Potter ad nauseam, or camping in the backyard. A *Say Yes to the Dress* marathon with decorate-your-own wedding cupcake bar. Cheap, easy, you'll hear giggles. And you'll be a hero.

Above all, hold your ground about whether or not you are inviting boys as well. If you decide to invite boys, call each of the parents and let them know it's co-ed, and when pickup time is. Often, tween girls are okay with boys there for a limited time. The boys may leave after the barbeque and the girls have a sleepover. Set clear boundaries with your daughter ahead of time and figure out if she wants to try to endorse them first and then lean on you, or if she wants you to be the "enforcer" from the get-go. It's entirely possible that your daughter will ask to either host or attend a co-ed slumber party in high school. This is entirely your decision, but we suggest you really use your network, talk about it with her mom if you are cooperative, and don't get coerced into hosting a party you're not comfortable with. Remember what we know about teen slumber parties. There is far more party than slumber. That means when you're likely asleep, they are likely awake. That essentially means there are hours when hormonal teens are in sleeping bags while you're snoring. We don't think we need to draw that picture any clearer. Besides your discomfort, we assure you that other parents will not feel comfortable, and some of the teens attending may not either. Best practice? Keep the overnighters single sex. We support all parents in protecting "girl-only" spaces, like slumber parties. Just as the space at a guy's campout is sort of sacred, we believe the same is true of the sacred teen girls' slumber party.

So get the food, help get some of the stuff (nail polish, glue, scissors and photos, a batch of cupcakes and frosting and sprinkles), rent the movies, add a bowl of M&M's, something to drink, maybe a pizza, and call it a party. Check in occasionally. Don't worry about being seen as a dorky dad who dances through the basement when they are cranking tunes, or who comes down in full vampire makeup while they're watching Twilight. Sure, you're embarrassing, but girls expect that from parents, and the other girls at the party will think you're funny and silly and that's currency for you with her friends. So have fun, don't be afraid to engage appropriately, and always keep the party safe. Don't supply alcohol. You know the reasons and you're smart enough to know the consequences and the laws.

CDS (Cool Dad Syndrome)

A quick word about wanting to be seen as the cool dad. Don't. For tween or teen girls, the definition of cool often includes things like poor boundaries (letting them watch any movie, break curfew, go out and not tell you where or with whom). Cool often means "things that Mom won't let me do." *Do not go there.*

The problem is that daughters will seem to crave a cool dad, reward a cool dad, and you will become more popular with some of her friends. On the flip side, you will become far less popular with other parents (your network), her teachers, and other parents who know what is likely to happen when cool dad is on duty. Cool dad lets boyfriends sleep over, lets kids go without information or contact with the supervising parents, drink in the basement. The father who is most vulnerable to this syndrome is the dad who is struggling with how to express his love for his daughter, or who wants to feel like he is "special" in her eyes. For some, it's easier to be the "good cop" who lets all kinds of things go by, rather than the "bad cop" who says no, holds the line, and can hold their position despite a tearful angry daughter. Cool dads will hear more "I love you daddy"s than the average dad, who is more likely to get some mixed emotions like anger at boundaries, or tears upon hearing that they cannot go to Montreal with their senior friends to that great concert. Cool dads tend to get cool because they aren't comfortable with setting boundaries and upholding them. Cool dads forget they are parents and not buddies. We all know that children, even teens, still need boundaries, and even though they won't tell us so, they crave them and feel safer when they're intact.

Kids who have lenient parents have often come to therapy as adults, stating they didn't feel very loved, cared about, or safe, running off the leash as they did. It's ironic. But the children who know that their dads were willing to be temporarily hated know that dad cared enough to say, "No. That's not a good decision. I love you enough to say no."

Maybe a better goal is "Slightly Dorky Dad." The dad who listens to current music, who jokes appropriately with the gaggle of teen girls who end up at the house after practice, who bakes the slightly floppy cupcakes with the team-colored frosting for the regionals, the dad who says, "No, no pierced noses at fourteen. You can hate me now. I'm good with that. Because deep down, you love me."

This dad goes on field trips even though he's the only dad. He goofs around at the barbeque and burns a few marshmallows in the s'mores while camping. He falls on his butt and laughs it off while chaperoning the ski trip. In short, the dorky dad participates, is present, and is not afraid to be, well, a dorky dad, not worrying about being the perfect dad, for the sake of being there.

You will find your new self, your best single dad. Don't worry about being the perfect dad; just be a good enough dad. You can do this.

Putting It All Together

So there you have it. It's just that simple. All you have to do as a single father to tween and teen girls is be a surrogate mom, a fashion consultant, a chauffeur, a coach, a well-behaved sideline parent, a volunteer, a chaperone, a dermatologist, an understanding friend, a hoop-shooting buddy, a leaning post, a listening ear, and a protector. Some us of expect teens to wear us out and give us a run for their money, hoping that at the other end of adolescence we'll be more than just a rung-out dishrag of a human. Not us. We want more than that. We want good, solid, healthy relationships with our daughters as we help them progress through their teen years.

You know how to throw a party, break up party, set limits about money and necklines, and be flexible about being challenged for your political leanings. You can stock the bathroom and know the differences between pads with wings and those that are extra-long. You have some idea about helping her with that big zit in the middle of her forehead, and you know that connection matters more to her than ever.

You're completely prepared to help her ease her cramps, quell her headaches, and lay on the couch with a heating pad when that's the best option. You have considered the possible ranges of her sexual identity formation, whether or not you will support her getting vaccinated against the human papillomavirus, how to gently raise and reraise the issue of sex.

You are aware of some of the warning signs of her stressors, from the lightweight to the scary, from zits to relationship violence. You have, by reading, allowed yourself to consider that your daughter might experience bullying, and you have bravely considered whether she might be bullying someone else.

At this moment, you're committed to working as well as you can with her mother. You won't freak out if she needs to talk to her mom when she's with you and you have some great ideas about how to stay connected to her when she's not with you.

If her mom is in the military and deployed overseas, you'll remember to keep her in the loop, to remember that she may notice changes in your daughter first, and not to shy away from conversations your daughter may want to have about how scary it is to have a mom in a warzone.

You're no stranger to the stages of grief and what's normal and complicated.

You have a bit more clarity about your own grief, and may even understand how important structure and keeping others close is to you and your children.

Most importantly, we sure hope that you have a greater sense, some confirmation, about how important your role is in the life of your daughter. You need not be perfect; you just need to be good enough, and that means being present, being willing to apologize when appropriate, to learn from and with your daughter, and to hold boundaries no matter how hard she cries and tells you she hates you.

So what now? Do you feel more comfortable when you pick her up at the end of a day, completely in control of the father-daughter situation? Do you have a greater comfort in the feminine product aisle?

We sincerely hope that you have a better sense of your daughter, and how you can be a great dad, during a really wonderful time of her life that has, frankly, gotten some really bad press. This can be an amazingly fun life stage for her, and for you. You can rise to the challenges and still enjoy the ride. There are no secrets to raising healthy kids; there is just common sense and good information. We hope we have given you a good start in getting some of the information you'll need.

Trust yourself. Trust your instincts. Understand the differences between listening and solving. Remember that your daughter really needs you involved in her life and caring about her on a day-to-day basis. Your healthy relationship with her is key to her long-term effectiveness as an adult woman. You matter every day.

Bibliography

"The Average American Woman—Dieting and Weight Statistics." Available online at www.inch-aweigh.com/dietstats.htm. Accessed October 18, 2011.

Baum, K., S. Catalano, M. Rand, and K. Rose. *Stalking Victimization in the United States*. Washington, DC: U.S. Department of Justice, Bureau of Justice Statistics, 2009.

Brizendine, Louann. *The Female Brain*. New York: Broadway Books, 2006.

———. *The Male Brain*. New York: Three Rivers Press, 2010.

Christ, G. H., K. Siegel, and A. E. Christ. "Adolescent Grief: It Never Really Hit Me . . . Until It Actually Happened." *JAMA* 288, no. 10 (September 11, 2002): 1269–78.

Cohen-Sandler, R. *Trust Me, Mom—Everyone Else Is Going!* New York: Penguin Books, 2003.

Craig, A. E. "Technology Keeps Deployed Mom Close to Family." *Charleston Daily Mail*, May 9, 2011.

Decker, M. R., J. G. Silverman, and A. Raj. "Dating Violence and Sexually Transmitted Disease/HIV Testing and Diagnosis among Adolescent Females." *Pediatrics* 116 (2005): 272–76.

Dellasega, C., and C. Nixon. *Twelve Strategies That Will End Female Bullying*. New York: Simon and Schuster, 2003.

Dempsey A. F., D. Singer, S. J. Clark, and M. Davis. "Parents' View on 3 Shot-Related Visits: Implications for Use of Adolescent Vaccines Like Human Papillomavirus Vaccine." *Academic Pediatrics* 9, no. 5 (September–October 2009): 348–52.

Doucet, A. "'Estrogen-Filled Worlds': Fathers as Primary Caregiver and Embodiment." *Sociological Review* 54, no. 4 (2006): 696–716.

"Eating Disorders Statistics." National Association of Anorexia Nervosa and Associated Disorders. Available online at www.anad.org/get-information/about-eating -disorders/eating-disorders-statistics. Accessed October 12, 2011.

Edelman, H. *Motherless Daughters*. New York: Bantam Doubleday Dell, 1994.

Elium, J., and D. Elium. *Raising a Daughter*. Berkeley, CA: Celestial Arts, 2003.

Faber, A., and E. Mazlish. *How to Talk So Teens Will Listen and Listen So Teens Will Talk*. New York: HarperCollins, 2006.

"Facts on American Teens' Sources of Information about Sex." Guttmacher Institute. February 2011. Available online at www.guttmacher.org/pubs/FB-Teen-Sex-Ed .html. Accessed October 18, 2011.

Fisher, E., and P. Halpern. *Dating for Dads*. New York: Bantam Books, 2008.

Fitzgerald, H. *The Grieving Teen*. New York: Simon and Schuster, 2000.

Glantz, A. "30,000 Single Mothers Deployed to Iraq, Afghanistan." *Huffington Post*, October 15, 2009.

Gorman, G. H., M. Eide, and E. Hisle-Gorman. "Wartime Military Deployment and Increased Pediatric Mental and Behavioral Health Complaints." *Pediatrics* 126, no. 6 (2010): 1058–66. Available online at http://pediatrics.aappublications.org/ content/early/2010/11/08/peds.2009-2856. Accessed October 18, 2011.

Health, United States, 2005: With Chartbook on Trends in the Health of Americans. Hyattsville, MD: National Center for Health Statistics, 2005.

Jarrell, A. "The Daddy Track." *Boston Globe Magazine*. August 8, 2007. Available online at www.boston.com/news/globe/magazine/articles/2007/07/08/the_ daddy_track. Accessed October 18, 2011.

Kaiser Family Foundation and Children Now. *Talking with Kids about Tough Issues: A National Survey of Parents and Kids*. Menlo Park, CA: Kaiser Family Foundation/ Children Now, 1999. Available partially online at www.kff.org/youthhivstds/ loader.cfm?url=/commonspot/security/getfile.cfm&PageID=14688. Accessed October 18, 2011.

Lynch, A., and L. Ashford. *How Can You Say That? Turning Hurtful Words into Conversations That Heal*. Middleton, WI: Pleasant Company Books, 2003.

McCarthy, M. *The Everything Guide to Raising Adolescent Girls*. Avon, MA: Adams Media, 2008.

McMahon, T. *Teen Tips: A Practical Survival Guide for Parents with Kids 11 to 19*. New York: Pocket Books, 1996.

McRee, A. L., N. T. Brewer, P. L. Reiter, S. L. Gottlieb, and J. S. Smith. "The Carolina HPV Immunization Attitudes and Beliefs Scale (CHIAS): Scale Development and Association with Intentions to Vaccinate." *Sexually Transmitted Diseases* 37, no. 4 (2010): 234–39.

Middleton, A., and K. Pfeifer. *Girl's Guide to Becoming a Teen*. New York: Jossey-Bass, 2006.

Musick, M. "When a Mother Is Deployed." *Mason Research*, March 15, 2011. Available online at http://masonresearch.gmu.edu/2011/03/when-a-mother-is-deployed. Accessed October 18, 2011.

Pierson, S., and P. Cohen. *You Have to Say I'm Pretty, You're My Mother: How to Help Your Daughter Learn to Love Her Body and Herself*. New York: Simon and Schuster, 2003.

Planned Parenthood of Northern New England. "Fact Sheet: Abortion Procedures and Anesthesia Options." PPNNE Form 301S 2/10 jkc.

"Puberty: Adolescent Female." Lucile Packard Children's Hospital at Stanford. Available online at www.lpch.org/DiseaseHealthInfo/HealthLibrary/adolescent/paf.html. Accessed October 18, 2011.

"Rape and Sexual Violence." National Institute of Justice. Available online at www.nij.gov/topics/crime/rape-sexual-violence. Accessed November 10, 2011.

Reiter, P. L., N. T. Brewer, S. L. Gottlieb, A. L. McRee, and J. S. Smith. "Parent's Health Beliefs and HPV Vaccination of Their Adolescent Daughters." *Social Science and Medicine* 69, no. 3 (August 2009): 475–80.

Rosario, M., J. Hunter, S. Maguen, M. Gwadz, and R. Smith. "The Coming-Out Process and Its Adaptational and Health-Related Associations among Gay, Lesbian, and Bisexual Youths: Stipulation and Exploration of a Model." *American Journal of Community Psychology* 29, no. 1 (2001): 133–60.

Rosario, M., E. W. Schrimshaw, and J. Hunter. "Predictors of Substance Use over Time among Gay, Lesbian and Bi-sexual Youth: An Examination of Three Hypotheses." *Addictive Behaviors* 29, no. 8 (November 2009): 1623–31.

Salamon, M. "Kids of Deployed Soldiers May Face More Mental Health Woes." *HealthDay*, November 8, 2010. Available online at www.abc12.com/story/13462892/kids-of-deployed-soldiers. Accessed October 18, 2011.

Savin-Williams, R. C. "Verbal and Physical Abuse as Stressors in the Lives of Lesbian, Gay Male, and Bisexual Youths: Associations with School Problems, Running Away, Substance Abuse, Prostitution and Suicide." *Journal of Clinical and Consulting Psychology* 62, no. 2 (April 1994): 261–69.

Snyderman, N. L., and P. Streep. *Girl in the Mirror*. New York: Hyperion Press, 2002.

"Teen Dating Violence." Centers for Disease Control and Prevention. Available online at www.cdc.gov/ViolencePrevention/intimatepartnerviolence/teen_dating_violence.html. Accessed October 12, 2011.

Walsh, D. *Why Do They Act That Way?* New York: Free Press, 2004.

Weitzman, S. *Not to People Like Us: Hidden Abuse in Upscale Marriages*. New York: Basic Books, 2000.

Willis, C. A. "The Grieving Process in Children: Strategies for Understanding, Educating and Reconciling Children's Perceptions of Death." *Early Childhood Education Journal* 29, no. 4 (2002): 221–26.

Wilson, E. "Children of Deployed More Likely to Seek Mental Health Care." *American Forces Press Service*, November 16, 2010. Available online at http://forum.navyadvancement.com/index.php/topic/70-children-of-deployed-more-likely-to-seek-mental-health-care. Accessed October 18, 2011.

Wiseman, R. *Queen Bees and Wannabes: Helping Your Daughter Survive Cliques, Gossip, Boyfriends and the New Realities of Girl World*. New York: Three Rivers Press, 2002.

"Youth Risk Behavior Surveillance." Department of Health and Human Services, Center for Disease Control and Prevention. 2009. Available online at www.cdc.gov/mmwr/pdf/ss/ss5905.pdf. Accessed October 18, 2011.

Additional Resources

Divorce

"Children and Divorce." AAMFT Consumer Update. Available online at www.aamft
.org/imis15/content/Consumer_Updates/Children_and_Divorce.aspx. Accessed
October 18, 2011.
"A Kid's Guide to Divorce." KidsHealth from Nemours. Available online at www
.kidshealth.org/kid/feeling/home_family/divorce.html. Accessed October 18, 2011.

Gay and Lesbian Issues

Bono, C. *Family Outing: A Guide to the Coming Out Process for Gays, Lesbians and
Their Families.* New York: Little, Brown, 2005.
Chase, C. *Queer 13: Lesbian and Gay Writers Recall Seventh Grade.* New York: Harp-
erCollins, 1999.
Gay, Lesbian and Straight Education Network. www.glsen.org.
Huegel, K. *GLBTQ: The Survival Guide for Gay, Lesbian, Bisexual, Transgender, and
Questioning Teens.* 2nd ed. Minneapolis: Free Spirit Publishing, 2011.
It Gets Better Project. www.itgetsbetter.org.
Marcus, E. *What If Someone I Know Is Gay? Answers to Questions about What It
Means to Be Gay and Lesbian.* New York: Simon Pulse, 2007.
Parents, Families and Friends of Lesbians and Gays. www.pflag.org.
Savage, D., and T. Miller. *It Gets Better: Coming Out, Overcoming Bullying and Creat-
ing a Life Worth Living.* New York: Dutton, 2011.

Media Literacy

Center for Media Literacy. www.medialit.org.
Cyberbullying.org. www.cyberbullying.org.

Mental Health

American Foundation for Suicide Prevention. www.afsp.org.
Depression Bipolar Support Alliance. www.dbsalliance.org.
National Association for Mental Illness. www.nami.org.

Military Deployment and Children

"How Deployment Stress Affects Children and Families: Research Findings." U.S.
Department of Veterans Affairs, National Center for PTSD. Available online

at www.ptsd.va.gov/professional/pages/pro_deployment_stress_children.asp. Accessed October 18, 2011.

The Soldiers Project. www.thesoldiersproject.org.

"Support for Military Children and Adolescents." American Academy of Pediatrics. Available online at www.aap.org/sections/uniformedservices/deployment/index .html. Accessed October 18, 2011.

Other Topics

Ginsburg, K., and M. Jablow. *Building Resilience in Children and Teens*. 2nd ed. Elk Grove Village, IL: American Academy of Pediatrics, 2011.

Hartley-Brewer, E. *Talking to Tweens: Getting It Right Before It Gets Rocky with Your 8- to 12-Year-Old*. New York: Basic Books, 2005.

LeBey, B. *Remarried with Children: Ten Secrets for Successfully Blending and Extending Your Family*. New York: Random House, 2005.

Shimberg, E. F. *Blending Families: A Guide for Parents, Stepparents, Grandparents, and Everyone Building a Successful New Family*. New York: Penguin, 1999.

Wisdom, S., and J. Green. *Stepcoupling: Creating and Sustaining a Strong Marriage in Today's Blended Family*. New York: Crown Publishing, 2002.

Index

abortion, 149–52

abuse, 10, 47, 144–47, 151, 159. *See also* bullying; stalking; teasing

acne, 39, 49, 82–83

addiction: alcohol, 100, 135; overdose from, 139, 141. *See also* substance use; suicide

adjustments, 11–12, 16–17, 25, 78, 85–91, 111; dad's dating-related, 106, 111; deployment, 25; shared custody, 85–91; transitioning from house to house, 11–12, 16–17

alcohol, 98–100, 135–37; dad's use of, 157–58; grief-related use of, 31–32; sexual assault and, 148; suicide and, 139–40, 144; Youth Risk Behavior Surveillance (YRBS), 46

allowances, 101–3

anniversary dates, 32, 34. *See also* grief and mourning; traditions

anorexia. *See* eating disorders: anorexia

antidepressants. *See* medications: antidepressants

anxiety, 10, 18, 24–25, 39, 68, 106, 111–12, 146

assault. *See* sexual assault

binging and purging. *See* eating disorders: binging and purging

birth control. *See* contraception

birthdays. *See* celebrations: birthdays

bisexuals, 141

blended families, 116–17

body image, 41, 127. *See also* eating disorders; growth and development; weight

boundaries: dad's dating-related, 112, 115; dating-related, 70–71, 97–98; ground rules of, 38–39, 74, 93–96; party-related, 160–63. *See also* consequences; limits; punishments; responsibilities; rules

boyfriends, 48, 71, 134, 143, 157–58, 161. *See also* dating

boys, 42, 45, 47, 98; dating, 70–74; friendship with, 68–69; teasing by, 83

bras, 19, 75–76, 78

breasts, 40–41, 49–50, 78. *See also* growth and development: physical

brothers. *See* siblings: brothers

bulimia. *See* eating disorders: bulimia

bullying, 46–47, 129–33, 145–46. *See also* abuse; stalking; teasing

burning. *See* self-injury

celebrations, 21, 87–89, 91, 117, 156, 159; birthdays, 86, 88–89, 117, 159;

About the Authors

Gretchen Gross is a clinical instructor in the Department of Psychiatry at the University of Vermont College of Medicine. She is also a clinician specializing in anxiety, depression, and bipolar disorder at the Mood and Anxiety Disorders Clinic, Department of Psychiatry at Fletcher Allen Health Care in Burlington, Vermont. In her private practice, she has counseled parents on issues related to divorce and parenting, communication, sexuality, and child rearing. She is a contributing author on sexuality in *Glass's Office Gynecology* and was on the review panel for the journal *Women in Therapy*. Each month, she contributes a column on life as a single mom called Solo Act to *Vermont Woman*. She has presented at national and international professional conferences on topics of reproductive decision-making, substance abuse, physicians and stress management, and teaching health professionals to feel more comfortable talking with and assessing clients for sexual dysfunction.

Patricia Livingston is a women's health nurse practitioner with more than twenty years of direct clinical experience at the University of Vermont (UVM) Center for Health and Wellbeing's Women's Health Clinic. She has counseled hundreds of young women in the areas of sexuality, relationship crises, and substance abuse. She has been a clinical preceptor to medical students, residents, and nurse practitioner students. She has been a guest lecturer in classrooms, dorms, and sororities and was a founding member of the UVM clinical team that established clinical protocol and policy for students identified with eating disorders.